TENCH

Jim Gibbinson

Beekay Publishers

Other angling titles by Beekay Publishers

Coarse

Carp Fever by Kevin Maddocks
The Art of Pole Fishing by Dickie Carr
Pike Fishing in the 80's by Neville Fickling
Basic Carp Fishing by Peter Mohan
Modern Specimen Hunting by Jim Gibbinson
Top Ten—tactics for the major species from ten leading anglers
Edited by Bruce Vaughan
Redmire Pool by Kevin Clifford & Len Arbery
Tactics for Big Pike by Bill Chillingworth
In Pursuit of Carp & Catfish by Kevin Maddocks
Cypry the Carp by Peter Mohan
The Beekay Guide to 450 Carp Waters
Jim Davidson Gets Hooked by Jim Davidson
In Pursuit of Predatory Fish by Neville Fickling
Tiger Bay by Rob Maylin
Understanding Barbel by Fred Crouch
Big-Water Carp by Jim Gibbinson
Mega-Pike by Eddie Turner

Sea

Boat Fishing at Sea by Phill Williams & Brian Douglas
Long Range Casting & Fishing Techniques by Paul Kerry
Cod Fishing by John Rawle
Uptide & Boatcasting by Bob Cox

Game

The Colour Guide to Fly-tying by Kevin Hyatt
Robson's Guide to Stillwater Trout Flies by Kenneth Robson
Dressed to Kill by Bob Carnill & Kenneth Robson

First published in 1990 by
BEEKAY PUBLISHERS
WITHY POOL, BEDFORD ROAD,
HENLOW CAMP, BEDS. SG16 6EA

© Beekay Publishers 1990

ISBN 0 947674 28 4

Typeset by BP Integraphics Ltd., Bath, Avon
Printed in Great Britain at The Bath Press, Avon

About the Author

Jim Gibbinson describes himself as 'a teacher by necessity and an angler by inclination'. That 'inclination' has led to him becoming something of an all-rounder, as happy casting to bass on an Irish surf-beach as trying to extract Kennet chub from beneath a winter flood-raft; but it is to gravel-pits that he is drawn most strongly. In this book he details his very individual approach to the pursuit of big tench—a pursuit that has been astonishingly successful with six tench over eight pounds and upwards of 50 over seven pounds to his credit! Jim attributes his remarkable success to the fact that he lives near some of the best tench waters in the country—but so do a lot of other anglers, yet very few of them come anywhere near matching Jim's results!

In addition to being one of the country's most successful tench anglers, Jim Gibbinson has caught carp to over 30 lb, pike to within ounces of 30 lb, bream to 9 lb 13 oz, chub to 5 lb 10 oz, eels to 5 lb 2 oz, crucian carp to 3 lb 4 oz, perch to 3 lb, roach to 2 lb 8 oz and rudd to 2 lb 2 oz. He has also caught bass to double-figures from the shore.

This is a very individual book by a very individual angler—Jim's approach and ideas are often controversial, but no one can argue with his results!

Acknowledgements

My thanks go to my many friends who, with their companionship and humour, greatly enhance the pleasure I get from my fishing—and who, when the necessity arises, are always ready to 'do the honours' with landing-net or camera.

My love and special thanks go to Maria who tolerates my bait-making, my anti-social hours and my long absences from home with equanimity—to her I dedicate this book ... and promise that I shall get round to the decorating one day!

Jim Gibbinson
Cuxton
March 1990

Contents

Drawings by the author
Photographs by the author and friends

Introduction

I have heard it said that nobody reads 'Introductions' to books—I hope that is not true because in this particular 'Introduction' I want to say a few things that I consider to be very important—in it I will outline the tone of the book, also its limitations; and most important of all, I want to give some advice regarding the welfare of the tench we catch.

I confess at the outset that I have mixed feelings about writing this book. First, I wonder about my credentials. Yes, I have caught a great many big tench, but to a large extent that is due to geographical good fortune in that I live near some of the finest big tench waters in the country. Also, my tench fishing experience is gravel-pit orientated. Yes, I have caught them from other waters, but not in any quantity because I am heart and soul a gravel-pit angler. You will not find advice in these pages on how to catch tench in small, lilied ponds, ornamental estate lakes or reed-lined canals—they are not my sort of waters. If, therefore, your tench fishing is mainly done in such waters you might find that much of what I write does not apply to you.

But my main concern is for the fishing itself. Tench are currently undergoing a dramatic increase in size, there have never been so many huge specimens awaiting capture as there are now—yet they are 'Cinderella' fish, they receive far less attention than they merit because they are overshadowed by carp. Everyone wants to be a carp angler—so tench are largely neglected. I applaud this situation. I prefer to fish for uncaught fish in quiet waters and I have no wish to see the situation change. But by writing this book might I contribute to tench becoming more popular? And by describing my methods and baits in detail, am I contributing to more tench being caught than would otherwise be the case?

The answer to both questions is probably, 'Yes'.

So how do I reconcile that belief with my conviction that fish thrive best on neglect—as do fisheries?

I cannot reconcile the conflict. I therefore spent a long time deciding whether or not I wanted to write this book at all. The fact that you are reading it, makes it obvious that I decided to go ahead—but I hope that it does not prove to be a decision that I come to regret. I love tench and tench fishing, and would hate to be instrumental in having an adverse effect on either the fish or the waters in which they live.

As a salve to my conscience, and in the hope that it might genuinely lead to captured tench being treated with care, I would like to make a few points concerning their welfare and protection.

Hooks should be small-barbed patterns. Tench are tough-mouthed and the tiniest barb will give adequate security. The patterns I use (and recommend in the appropriate chapters) are small-barbed patterns—if alternative patterns are used please ensure that the barb is filed down small. A large barb is likely to cause damage when it is removed from the fish's mouth—damage that can cause ulceration and subsequent erosion which, in turn, leads to those awful examples of 'parrot mouth'.

Tench should *never* be retained in a keepnet. In fact, I will go further and say that *no* fish should be retained in a keepnet—ever. The abolition of keepnets would be a major conservation measure and would lead to a dramatic improvement in the condition and survival rate of captured fish. Yes, it would mean an end to conventional match-fishing – but the practice of retaining fish in keepnets is completely indefensible and we have to decide which is more important, match-fishing or conservation. My answer is, 'No contest'—in more ways than one.

Tench should not, in fact, be retained at all. If *short-term* retention is deemed necessary, while a camera is set up for example, a keepsack (carp-sack) should be used, but only for a very short while. In very hot conditions, such as that fantastic summer of '89, do not even contemplate retaining any fish for longer than 5 or 10 minutes; in such conditions the margins become seriously depleted of oxygen and I know of several instances of both tench and carp that died in such circumstances.

Only one fish should be placed in a keepsack at a time. Apart from the adverse effects of 2 or more fish competing for limited oxygen, those same 2 or more fish struggling as they are lifted from the water are likely to sustain damage.

To weigh fish, use a proper weigh-sling (Kevin Nash's weigh-slings, and his carp-sacks, are ideal—I recommend them unreservedly). The weigh-sling should be pre-wetted before a fish is placed inside, as should sacks. A weigh-sling also provides a safe and secure means of carrying a tench to the water's edge prior to its return. A tench carried in the angler's hands could suddenly struggle and fall from his (or her) grasp —with obvious risk of injury.

Never, ever lay a tench on hard ground—you can buy proper unhooking mats and one angler I know carries a small piece of 'Dunlopillo' carpet underlay on which to lay his fish, but I always manage to find a nice soft patch of grass or clover, or failing that I make a sort of grass 'nest' in one corner of my pitch and on top of this I put a wet keepsack (I picked up this tip from Brian Mills—it works perfectly).

Finally, remember that the best conservation measure of all is clean water and water availability. Tench, it is true, are not generally fish of rivers (although some rivers hold viable numbers of them), but all anglers, whatever species they fish for, should support and be members of the ACA (the Anglers' Cooperative Association). Membership only costs a few pounds a year, little more than 2 or 3 pints of maggots or a pack of ready-made boilies, so please lend them your support. You will find their address at the end of this 'Introduction'.

Pollution, of the sort that affects rivers, is rarely a problem in still-waters—although there can be problems from silage seepage and from eutrophication—but a major problem is that of backfilling. Unfortunately there are no 'watchdog' bodies to help us fight proposed backfilling projects—but we can have allies if we use our commonsense and present a united front. Look at it this way—if a backfilling project is only likely to upset a few anglers there is every likelihood that it will go ahead. But supposing the anglers ally themselves with other interested parties—the RSPB and other bird-watching groups, local footpath groups, nature conservancy groups (and *the* Nature Conservancy for that matter) and, heaven help us, wind-surfers and related pond-admirals(!) ... Combine that lot and you are starting to get what looks like a powerful lobby are you not? We may not relish the prospect of sharing our waters with wind-surfers and the like; but I would far rather share my water than have it backfilled and converted to an industrial estate or refuse tip.

It makes sense does it not?

And let us do our part by demonstrating that we are a responsible body of people – let us take our rubbish home and take great care not to endanger wildlife by discarding mono. Only by behaving in an exemplary manner can we divert or offset some of the anti-angling feeling that is a legacy of the lead-shot and swans issue. I feel that we came in for a greater proportion of the blame than we merited in that particular saga—but whatever your personal feelings on the matter, please ensure that all restrictions on the use of lead are conscientiously observed.

Now, here is that address I promised you – they do a marvellous job on our behalf, so please help them to continue with the fight against water pollution by joining. The annual subscription is only £5 ... it is not a lot to ask, is it?

Anglers' Cooperative Association
23 Castlegate
Grantham
Lincs
NG31 6SW

Time and Season

It is an unfortunate fact of life that when the season opens in mid-June few tench will have finished spawning; if the spring has been a cold one (a common occurrence in recent years, with the notable exception of 1989) they may not have even *started* spawning. Early season tench fishing will, therefore, inevitably produce a high proportion of females carrying spawn, some will be heavily laden with spawn. I do not intend discussing the ethics of fishing for spawny tench because it would inevitably develop into a more general discussion on the merits or otherwise of our existing close-season. It would be difficult anyway to offer meaningful protection to tench because they tend to spawn over a protracted period of time, often seeming to make several attempts and shedding a proportion of their spawn at each attempt. So even if we delay our tench fishing until mid-July, we will still catch a number of spawny fish—or, at least, fish that show all the outward signs of carrying spawn.

Few tench anglers would willingly delay the start of their fishing because it would drastically shorten the productive period. There is little doubt that on the vast majority of waters the best of the season's fishing is over by mid-August. Many tench anglers will claim that I have been excessively generous in that statement and will claim the best is over long before mid-August; only recently I was talking to a very successful tench angler who reckons that the best is over by the end of June!

I would modify his assessment by saying that the *easiest* fishing is often over by the end of June, but *good* tench fishing continues at least until the end of July. Worthwhile fishing continues until at least the middle of August—and beyond if the weather is warm and settled.

September and October are strange months for tench. There *can* be a silly period of a couple of weeks in early autumn when tench feed well—but in recent seasons this does not seem to have been the regular occurrence that it used to be. What has tended to happen recently is that there has been a sudden and dramatic 'switch-off' at the tail-end of August or maybe early in September after which, although tench continue to roll regularly, very few are caught. This happens even on heavily stocked waters—I could take you to a medium sized gravel-pit that is

I get very few of these—it is an evening capture and I am looking very worried in case the self-take picture doesn't come out!

absolutely heaving with tench, and they are a great frustration to the carp anglers on the water because any attempt to lace a swim with particles results in hoards of tench invading the pitch and behaving for all the world like ravenous piranhas! But come late August and the change is incredible—they continue to show readily but very, very rarely pick up a bait.

Winter tench fishing is of considerable academic interest but is not, in my opinion, really worthwhile. I say that despite having caught numerous tench in winter, including some big ones to 7 lb plus, but if my life depended on my catching a tench I certainly would not attempt to do it in the winter! I can recall periods in some waters when winter tench fishing has been both reliable and productive, but such occasions tend to be 'one-offs' and do not repeat themselves on an annual basis. I am aware that there are idiosyncratic waters, in fact I know one water that rarely produces tench before Christmas, but exceptions should not be given disproportionate emphasis or the overall picture becomes distorted.

Tench are first and foremost fish of high summer. Exceptions do not disprove that rule.

Feeding Times

According to traditional angling literature, the classic feeding times are early morning and late evening—and such may be the best times in ponds, estate lakes and canals (I don't know because I do not fish for tench in such waters)—but they are not generally the best times for tench in gravel pits.

I like to arrive at dawn, or maybe a little before, but not because I anticipate early morning feeding, it is to increase the chances of getting the swim I want. It also enables me to get the swim baited and give it a chance to quieten down ready for the beginning of the first feeding spell.

Occasionally I catch an early fish, but normally I expect the first take to come sometime between 7.00 am and 9.00 am. If I catch a fish during that period I am very hopeful of another 1 or 2 before lunchtime, and I remain confident until about midway through the afternoon. If, however, that 7.00 am to 9.00 am period passes without a take I will probably move to another pitch, especially if I have seen no sign of rolling fish nor received line-bites.

If I am going to catch at all, I expect to have done so by about 3.30 pm. The latter part of the afternoon I do not rate very highly—and I like evenings even less. I've caught tench late in the afternoon, I've caught them in the evenings too, but taken overall they are not productive times.

Both of these were caught before going to work in the morning—and both topped
7 lb.

This feeding 'timetable' is unfortunately irreconcilable with normal work times. I am a teacher and have to be at school by about 8.30 am. Early morning, pre-work sessions therefore have to end by 7.30 am at the very latest—and most mornings that is just about when I am getting keyed-up ready for the first take! Just occasionally I manage to squeeze in a fish or 2, but most days I am having to pack up just as the first fish decides to roll over the groundbait—it is most frustrating.

A succession of early mornings, each followed by a full day's work, is pretty debilitating too—and to make matters worse it is my busiest time of year what with tests, assessments and report-writing. So, in an effort to preserve my health and sanity I often try the altogether easier option of after-work sessions. Trouble is, I usually arrive at the water just after the day's feeding has ended!

So for the first few weeks of the season I am restricted to weekends —and that in turn makes swim-choice a problem because most of the waters I fish for tench are popular carp waters too—as a result they are well and truly 'stitched up' from Friday evening through to Sunday evening.

I relate that tale of woe not to elicit sympathy (although it wouldn't come amiss!) but to let you know that I understand and share the same frustrations and difficulties as everyone else. And that point is made to reassure you that the things I write are relevant to everyone who reads this. There is a popular notion that angling authors live some sort of rarified existence whereupon they fish practically full-time (presumably financed by magazines, bait-firms etc)—and furthermore, their fishing is done in exclusive, private waters where there is no competition for swims.

If only it were so!

The bulk of my tench fishing is done in day-ticket and commercial fisheries—waters that are open to everyone (and indeed, sometimes it looks as though everyone has decided to turn up!). They are superb waters, but their popularity means that swim choice can be very restricted, especially during the first two or three weeks of the season.

To mitigate this problem I sometimes try to get to the water as soon as I possibly can on a Friday evening—I finish work at about 4.00 pm and can thus sometimes get the pitch I want before the weekend crowds arrive. As I am at the water anyway, I put out baits. But in truth I have found night fishing to be very nearly a complete waste of time. I catch the occasional tench after dark, but they really are exceptions. Most times I get an uninterrupted night's sleep and have to wait until after sunrise for my first fish.

The situation changes somewhat after mid-August when night feeding becomes much more evident; it can even be the best time—not often, but it can.

One that was taken during a pre-work morning session.

In order of preference, then, here is my personal list of tench feeding times:

1. morning 7.00 am to 12.00 noon
2. early afternoon 12.00 noon to 3.30 pm
3. early morning dawn to 7.00 am
4. late afternoon 3.30 pm to 6.00 pm
5. evening 6.00 pm to dusk
6. night

What I have written thus far applies to the normal tench season (mid-June to late August); outside of that period I have insufficient experience to offer really reliable advice. Such experience as I do have, coupled with the anecdotal experience of friends, suggests that during autumn, night fishing becomes much more worthwhile, necessary even.

My experience of winter tench fishing (deliberate and accidental) suggests that the afternoon is best, particularly about 3.00 pm. I have, however, reliable reports from some friends that after-dark fishing in winter can be productive, even in bitterly cold conditions with the water temperature in the high 30's Fahr (approximately 3 to 4 °C). I recall Bob Morris telling me how he and his father caught regularly from a small gravel pit by fishing maggots in maggot-baited pitches after dark—they caught in bitterly cold conditions and only had their fishing guillotined by the lake icing over!

I have not tried after-dark tench fishing in winter so cannot speak from personal experience, but the experience of Bob and his father, coupled with that of a few other anglers whose judgement I respect, convinces me that it *can* be a viable proposition—and can be worthwhile even on cold, frosty nights with cat-ice in the margins.

But I am not sufficiently convinced to want to try it for myself!

Don't forget — discarded line kills birds and other wild animals

Tench Weather

Gravel-pit tench love heatwave conditions. If I could choose my weather for tench fishing I would choose a 'factor-six day'—the sort of day that demands high factor sun-cream on all exposed skin. The marvellous summer of '89, for example, was the best tench season I can recall. 1988, by contrast, was cool—the tench fishing that year was poor. There was a short spell in August that boasted a few consecutive hot days and by the end of that few-day period the tench were feeding well—then cool weather returned and the tench fishing reverted to being poor again.

As well as influencing their willingness to feed, temperature has a considerable effect on *where* they feed. If I had to identify just one key piece of advice it would be this:

'When it's hot—fish close;

When it's not—don't!'

Not the most poetically expressed piece of advice you could be offered, I agree, but certainly one of the most important.

My concept of 'close-in' is obviously at variance to that of most other anglers though—when they have asked me why my indicators keep rattling off and their's do not, I have told them about fishing close when the weather and water are warm, but their close-in rod has invariably been further out than my furthest would be.

So, for 'close-in', perhaps you had better substitute, 'ever so, ever so close-in!'

'It's all very well on his waters', some of you are doubtless thinking, 'but it wouldn't work on ours.'

Possibly there are exceptions, but in all the waters I have fished, the 'rule' has applied. Remember though, not all margins are at the edge of the main bank—there are island margins too, and the same 'rule' applies to them.

The cooler it gets, however, the less productive do the margins become—in prolonged cool conditions I would probably ignore the margins completely.

But back to my hot, sunny day. Ideally it would be accompanied by a nice breeze, preferably a southerly, the sort that feels as though

Shorts and sun-cream—perfect tench weather.

A 6 lb male tench taken in heatwave conditions.

it has come from an oven-extractor. A south-easterly is nearly as good—in fact the best morning's tench catch I ever made, 4 over 7 lb (one of which weighed over 8 lb) was taken during a hot, sunny, south-easterly.

The south-westerly tends to be cooler, it is often cloudy and can sometimes be wet. It can be good but is better for carp and bream than for tench.

The anti-cyclonic summer easterly is usually good—the high pressure accompanying it not being the debit with tench that it is with carp and bream.

The wet westerly is not particularly good. The north-westerly is poor.

I would far rather have a sunny, flat-calm than a cloudy day with a cool wind.

I have heard it said that tench like thunderstorms.

I hate them!

I have fished through thunderstorms but have yet to catch a tench while doing so—mind you, while sitting there with the rain falling in torrents and lightning flashing all around me, I would not strike a run even if one occurred. I have absolutely no intention of holding an 11 or 12 foot carbon lightning-conductor while a storm is in progress. Think about it for a moment. Carbon fibre is a good conductor of electricity—so surely it would be dangerous to hold a carbon rod in a storm. I have never heard or seen any other reference to the potential danger of so doing—and maybe there is a physicist out there who reckons I am over-stating the danger ... okay chum—*you* put it to the test, because I sure as hell do not intend to do so!

There is evidently a simple calculation, by means of which it is possible to calculate how far away each lightning flash occurs. As far as I remember you count elephants from the flash to the thunderclap ... 'one elephant, two elephants' etc—this apparently being a fairly accurate way of counting seconds. You then divide by five. I can never remember whether the result is in miles or kilometres, but I am always immensely reassured by a time delay that permits a reasonable count. But when the flash and the bang come simultaneously I do not need calculations of any sort to convince me that it is too damn close!

From which you may conclude that I have an irrational fear of thunderstorms.

Okay—so what is irrational about not wanting to be welded to my chair by 20 trillion volts?

That's a wholly justified and rational fear in my book!

Tackle

Rods

It is difficult to give advice on rods because individual preferences vary so much—I, for example, like tip-actioned, semi fast-taper designs, but many experienced tench anglers prefer softer, through-action models. I generally use 11 footers (for legering), but here I am in a minority because there is no doubt that 12 footers are far more popular.

Who is right?

We all are! So when I detail my preferences, please remember that choice is dictated by personal taste as much as by efficiency. And do not imagine for one moment that your rods, if they differ from mine, are unsuitable. If you like them—they are suitable. It is as simple as that. But for those who would like more detailed recommendations, I shall describe the rods I use.

A full tench armoury would, ideally, comprise a float-rod and 2, maybe 3 different weight leger-rods.

As I do so little float fishing I am not really qualified to make worthwhile recommendations. I cannot remember the last tench I caught on float tackle, but it would certainly have been at least 5 or 6 seasons ago—so obviously I am not the man to give up-to-the-minute advice on float-rods. I am not trying to be cavalier—just honest.

But leger-rods are another matter because I am essentially a leger-angler. For feeder-fishing and general light-legering (line up to 6 lb test, but more usually 4 to 5 lb test) I like an 11 ft model with a test-curve of about 1¼ lb. I prefer 11 ft rods because so much of my tench fishing is done in swims where extra length would be a liability due to overhead branches and the proximity of bushes or high banks just behind the pitch. I can think of some swims where even 11 footers are inconveniently long—but on balance I think they are the best compromise.

For big fish in very weedy swims I prefer something a bit heavier—my choice being an 11 ft, 1¾ lb test-curve, light carp rod. Some anglers might regard such a rod as being too heavy for tench, but I would respond by saying that the rod needs to match the line, and for most of my tench

A big tench laying on the carp-sack in which it has been briefly retained. Carp-sacks are far superior to keepnets.

fishing I regard 9 lb test line as essential—and 9 lb line partners my 1¾ lb test-curve rods beautifully.

The heaviest rods I use for tench are 2¼ lb test-curve, general-purpose carp rods; they are used relatively seldom but are necessary in those swims where the weed is really horrendous and line of 11 or 12 lb test is essential to ensure that fish are not lost.

There are a lot of good rods to choose from these days, ranging from up-market models costing upwards of £100 each to budget buys costing less than half that figure. All those from reputable manufacturers are made from good quality blanks so the main deciding factor is likely to be the depth of your pocket. There *are* differences in the quality of the raw materials used in rods from different price-brackets, but in practical terms I doubt that performance differences are likely to be very significant—if indeed they are even discernible. The most obvious differences are likely to be in the quality of the fittings rather than the performance characteristics of the blanks.

Line

In deciding how strong a line to use, we have to consider how tench behave when hooked. They are powerful fish that fight deep; they rarely embark on irresistible reel-screetching runs even when hooked on light tackle; that is not their style, instead they hug the bottom and are adept at finding any weed that is in the proximity. And no other fish is as difficult to shift from weed as is a tench. I honestly regard a 5 lb tench as a more difficult prospect to shift from a weedbed than is a carp of 20 lb plus. That is because a carp, on getting its 'second-wind', will fight its own way free. But a tench will just lay there. No matter how long you wait, no matter if you pull and heave, or allow slack—that tench will not move. The only way to shift them is to heave sufficiently hard to pull them free of the weed, or to detach the chunk of weedbed in which the tench is lying. It is not a pretty way of playing fish and I have lost count of the number of times I have pulled in a mass of weed with a tench's tail wagging gently from the back-end of it. On parting the weed there lies revealed a magnificent 6 or 7 lb tench that, with its eyes covered, has come in without a wriggle ... but once clear of the weed they proceed to go berserk!

So, the line must be strong enough to haul them in bodily if they become weeded, and strong enough to hold them free of weed if circumstances permit. Hence my earlier mention of 9 lb line—this being my usual choice for weedy swims. Sometimes I go even heavier and there are a couple of swims in one particular water where I use 11 lb test—cringe if you will, but I can assure you that there have been times when I have been glad of it.

For feeder-fishing and light/medium legering in open water I generally use 4 or 5 lb test.

The brand I usually use is Sylcast—frankly I think they owe me something in royalties because I have been recommending this line for many years—I suspect that I was instrumental in bringing about its current popularity because when I first used and recommended it, it was generally considered to be a cheap 'ditter's-line'. So, if Mr Sylcast is riding around in a Mercedes, he knows who he has got to thank for it!

Recently I have tried Brent nylon which, frankly, I find indistinguishable from Sylcast. It is cheaper too.

Other lines I use with confidence are Bayer, Maxima and Drennan Super-Specimen. This particular threesome strike me as being identical too—but different from Sylcast and Brent.

For the whole of last season I used the new ultra-soft HPPE (High Performance Polethylene) braids, 'Silkworm' and 'Gamabraid', for hook-links. The difference in diameter between 7 lb-ish and 15 lb was so slight I felt I may as well have the added strength and security of the heavier stuff. I was very impressed and recommend it for all heavy fishing. For light to medium work, such as feeder fishing, I still use mono.

Bleep! All set—now it is up to the tench to do their bit!

Reels

For 90% of my tench fishing I use Mitchell 410A's. They are reliable, functional and have a superb after-sales back-up. I have played with some of the opposition's models and whilst acknowledging that there are some lovely examples of engineering around, many of the high-tech reels currently available strike me as being out of proportion. They seem to be needlessly big and heavy for the job they are required to do. So, to date I have found nothing to rival my 410A's—I do not claim that they are perfect but I reckon they are the best currently available.

Bite Indicators

I used to use Delkim converted Optonics, but, following the High Court action in which Delkim (Del Romang) was taken to court by Dellareed (the manufacturers of Optonics) and prevented from undertaking any more conversions, I sold them. I did so because I disagreed very strongly with Dellareed's action and decided that I no longer wished to be seen using their products—to be seen using them is, after all, a sort of endorsement is it not?

My present set of alarms are some that I privately commissioned—they are not generally available so there is no point in my giving further details.

Of the 'off-the-peg' models nowadays available I am not qualified to pass comment—I have not used them so have no way of knowing how effective and reliable they are.

I am sorry to be so negative, but the present situation as regards bite-alarms is not a particularly helpful one to the angler—the choice is very limited and legal constraints inhibit development.

Don't blame me—I went to the High Court to have my say on the matter but, unfortunately, Del Romang (on whose behalf I appeared) lost the case.

Although I have included electronic devices in this 'Bite Indicators' section, they are not really indicators at all, but alarms. The true indicators are those that act on a 'bobbin' principle—and one of the simplest of those is the ring-bobbin. This is made from aquarium air-pipe tubing (or aero-modellers' fuel-pipe tubing—it is the same stuff). The drawing is self-explanatory (Fig. 1).

Normally I hang a ring-bobbin between the butt-ring and second-ring, and slide it over a double-ended knitting-needle to prevent it swinging in the wind (Fig. 2).

It is used with the pick-up of the reel closed and with the anti-reverse mechanism disengaged (i.e. in 'spin').

It is a sensitive, neat and practical arrangement and works very well.

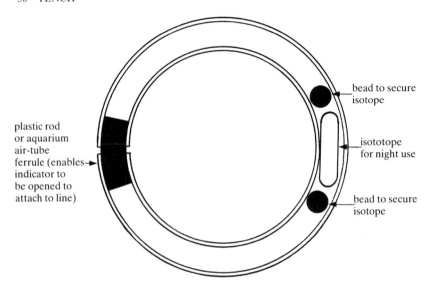

plastic rod
or aquarium
air-tube
ferrule (enables→
indicator to
be opened to
attach to line)

bead to secure
isotope

isototope
for night use

bead to secure
isotope

Fig. 1. Bobbin-type ring indicator.

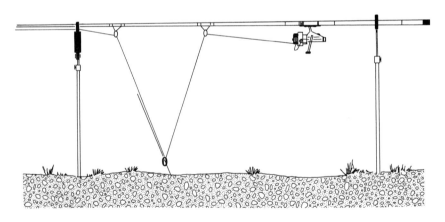

Fig. 2. Ring-bobbin on needle to prevent it swinging in the wind.

It is my usual choice when feeder fishing or light legering; methods that are best employed with a closed pick-up to allow an instant strike.

When I am fishing heavy, usually a sort of modified carp-style, I have the bale-arm of the reel open, and for open-spool methods nothing

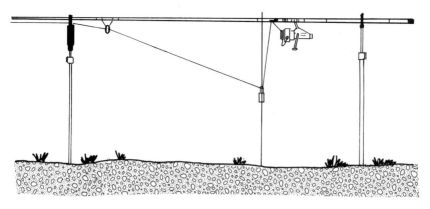

Fig. 3. Monkey-climber set to show drop-backs as well as runs.

beats a monkey-climber. There are many variations in use and most accessory manufacturers have their own particular version. I get the feeling
that my brother Rick, who invented the monkey-climber, rather missed
the boat with this idea. If he had patented the idea and allowed manufacturers to make them under licence he might now be living in a pent-house
apartment and going fishing in a Ferrari ... well, not quite perhaps, but
I reckon he would have done quite well out of it. But Rick is not commer-
cially-minded, nor, indeed, am I—or we would have become a bait-com-
pany years ago!

I guess that neither of us want the hassle of being angling-entrepre-
neurs. Besides, success in business demands commitment—and the only
commitments Rick and I want are to our families and our fishing. The
entrepreneurs are welcome to the constant pressure of chasing-up recalci-
trant payers and the 'joys' of VAT returns.

I still think Rick should have patented the monkey-climber though!

Of the commercial versions available I use two: the Gardner 'Grease
Monkey' for close-to-medium range work, and the Mickey Sly model
when I am fishing at longer range and want one that effectively shows
drop-backs (Fig. 3).

Rod-Rests

A good set of rod-rests is essential—I like bank-stick/buzzer-bar combinations because on many gravel-pits it is something of an achievement
to get 2 rests in the hard stony banks, let alone 4 (or 6, if 3 rods are
used). The best bank-stick/buzzer-bar sets I have ever used have been
those made by Chris Brown—I bought mine about a year ago and having

found them ideal in every way, wonder why on earth I tolerated inferior and less efficient set-ups for so long. They are larger in diameter than other bank-sticks which, as well as making them very sturdy, eliminates twisting—something to which other buzzer-bar set-ups are prone. You can get anti-twist stabilisers of various kinds, but with Chris's bank-sticks you do not need them.

Another feature of Chris's set-up is that the design of the buzzer-bar enables it to be used to force a bank-stick into an obstinate bank. Try this with other buzzer-bars and they will bend.

Needle-bar clamps that enable indicator needles to be attached to the bank-stick, rather than stuck in the ground, are a useful idea—it often being impossible to position the needles where you want them due to stones and rocks impeding penetration. The needle-bar obviously has to be compatible with the bank-stick so, inevitably, I acquired Chris Brown's version. At the risk of this sounding like a Chris Brown benefit (and for the benefit of cynics among you I would make the point that I bought my sticks, bars and clamp from Bob Morris and paid the normal going rate. Okay?) I will say that it is the best I have seen.

Where banks are difficult to the point of being impossible, or where the fishing is being done from wooden platforms, jetties or tarmacadam paths, a rod-pod is a boon. The Gardner model is inexpensive and is a good, workmanlike piece of kit. There are some higher-priced state-of-the-art models around too, but I have not tried them so am not qualified to pass comment. I have heard good reports though, especially of the KJB model.

Not being one of those anglers who loads himself like a pack-horse and is prepared to make several trips to-and-from the car park, I did not want to have one set of bank-sticks/buzzer-bars for normal use and a completely different set of rests for when I needed to use a 'pod' or stand, so while talking to Bob Morris one day I suggested that he contact Chris Brown with a view to Chris producing some sort of compatible 'pod' arrangement. A couple of weeks later I received a 'phone call from Bob, telling me that Chris had delivered a prototype 'pod' to him for me to try. The 'pod' was a one-off and I am not sure if Chris intends producing it commercially or not—but he ought to. It is without doubt the most versatile and stable 'pod' arrangement I have ever seen. And for those to whom such things are important I will add in passing that it well and truly looks 'the biz!'

And to think, I promised myself I would never use that phrase!

Chairs

I often use an adjustable-leg bed-chair, especially in nice weather when I tend to lay back in the sunshine and relax with a book. I also use

Seven pounds – another run occurred while this picture was being taken. That was over 7 lb too!

8 lb 5 oz, my second biggest – it took particles in the margins.

8 lb 6 oz, my best ever.

A gorgeous looking seven-plus is returned to the water.

Part of a nine-fish catch on boilies. They were not weighed but they averaged six-ish

8 lb 2 oz – the biggest of an astonishing four-fish catch in a day, they were all over 7 lb!

Eight-plus to particles fished at maximum particle range.

Eight plus – and remarkable in that it was caught in the evening and over blanket-weed; both unusual occurrences in my experience.

The first of the day—a big tench that fell to feeder tackle is netted.

the bed-chair for overnight sessions but, for reasons explained elsewhere, do comparatively few of those.

For short sessions of just a few hours, or when the weather is such that I am not likely to want to lay back and sun-bathe, I use a small folding chair. Actually I use two (but only one at a time, you understand!). The first is a Lafuma beach-chair which, although super-comfortable, is only suitable for nice level banks. The other is the much more versatile adjustable-leg Cliff Fox model. The Lafuma model has the edge when it comes to comfort, but if I were restricted to just one I would unhesitatingly choose Cliff Fox's because it can be levelled no matter what the configuration of the bank.

Sundries

Of umbrellas I shall say little. They are a necessary evil. I generally use a 45 in nylon model for day fishing and the big Nashy oval version for night sessions.

I never use holdalls. My rods are carried tackled-up and are held together with home-made rod-bands (I suspect that I invented these but

A big tench is landed from a gravel-pit. As can be clearly seen, it fell to feeder tackle.

will refrain from blowing my trumpet too enthusiastically ... after all, they hardly qualify as the most brilliant of concepts, do they? I would not have mentioned it at all were it not for a pathetic need to claw some credibility ...). The net-pole is attached to the rods by the rod-bands too.

Bank-sticks, net arms and umbrella are carried in a sling—unless I am fishing those waters where car break-ins are a very high risk, in which case I go by bike. Attaching gear to a bike is something of an art and something in which I can claim quite a high level of expertise, but I shall not enlarge on the subject because it would be of interest to so few readers. It is worth consideration if you live fairly near your waters though, and enables you to enjoy your fishing without worrying that a bunch of Neanderthal numbskulls are abusing your car. Unfortunately it is a fact of life that a lot of our choices are influenced by the activities of socially cretinous unbalanced morons (SCUM).

I shall not list all the odds-and-ends and accessories that I use because it would end up being an excessively long list, many will be mentioned

Two of seven-plus taken on feeder tackle.

elsewhere where relevant anyway, but there is one accessory that is so useful that it deserves special emphasis.

High factor sun-cream.

No, I am not being flippant—I am being serious. Some of the best days for tench are the hottest and sunniest of which our climate is capable—and sitting out in intense sunshine is potentially dangerous. As well as short-term sunburn, we risk long-term skin-cancer. So, if you cannot sit in the shade on such days, use sun-cream, at least factor six. If you are fair-skinned and prone to burning, use a higher factor, total sun-block may even be necessary.

Ultra-violet and infra-red can also damage your eyes, so a pair of sunglasses offering high-level protection are necessary too (remember, the effects of sunlight are magnified when we are near water because of the high proportion of light that is reflected).

Having said that I would mention one accessory, I have mentioned 2! I shall now compound the error by mentioning a few more ... all have a common theme though, that of personal comfort and welfare.

I always carry a mini first-aid kit containing: Paracetamol (or Aspirin), some plasters, diarrhoea tablets, sting-relief and anti-histamine tablets. The last-named are a relatively recent acquisition and are the result of having been stung on the hand by a wasp last summer. My hand ballooned alarmingly (and hurt like hell). I subsequently caught a 7 lb plus tench and a near 20 lb carp but could barely hold the rod to play them. The incident convinced me, if I needed convincing, that if ever I am unfortunate enough to be stung on the throat or front part of my neck I shall seek immediate medical help—a throat or neck swelling could be extremely dangerous if it resulted in blocked air passages.

Which brings me to the subject of Weil's disease. Many angling waters have a rat population, and some female rats are capable of transmitting Weil's disease in their urine. So *never* drink lake or river water (unless it has been well-boiled, and frankly I would not do it even then) and try to prevent cuts and scratches being immersed.

If you get 'flu-type symptoms in summer it is worth going to a doctor and explaining that you are concerned that you may have contracted Weil's disease. Make no mistake, Weil's disease is a killer—early diagnosis and treatment increase the chances of recovery but due to its comparative rarity, correct diagnosis sometimes comes too late for treatment to be effective. So do not delay—if you are worried, see your doctor.

Location

Let me emphasise at the outset that what follows draws on my experience with gravel-pits. To what extent my observations will apply to other sorts of waters I do not know. I suspect that the application to other waters will be very limited, although there is bound to be some overlap of course.

Before I describe those physical features that seem to be liked by tench, I think it is important to make a few general observations regarding their movements and behaviour.

Tench do not allow themselves to be shepherded about a water by conditions of wind and temperature as, for example, do carp—they tend, instead, to take up residence in particular areas, often quite 'tight' areas. After a few weeks they will move, and when they do they will do so en-masse. These movements are seasonal and are relatively unaffected by changing weather conditions.

Sometimes the arrival and subsequent departure of the fish can be predicted with considerable accuracy—the pattern being duplicated every season. An outcome of this on certain well-known tench waters is that some swims are 'stitched up' for weeks on end by a group of friends fishing a sort of rota system. Sometimes there is a sort of queueing or 'stacking' system in operation—while popular early-season swims can be occupied (and thus reserved) for a week or more before the season begins!

It is a lunatic situation and whilst it undoubtedly leads to the capture of some very big tench, it is hardly very satisfying nor, for that matter, very difficult fishing—the main requirement being that you are capable of withstanding long sessions without becoming bored out of your skull. If the only ones to suffer were unimaginative anglers it would not matter—but unfortunately this situation is very bad for the tench. Tench do not seem to respond to pressure by moving—the result being that the same fish are caught over and over again. Inevitably they become damaged which is characterised in extreme cases by ulceration and erosion around the mouth and the subsequent development of 'beak mouth'. Bruising and fin-damage occur too. Human nature being what it is, known hot-spots are not going to be left alone no matter how badly the fish suffer.

I find this very sad and would welcome the establishment of no-fishing exclusion-zones on waters where this sort of thing is a problem. Yes, it would mean that fewer big tench were caught, but ultimately it would benefit the fish.

Sadly, tench are victims of their own predictability—it is therefore up to us to accord them protection in those waters that are heavily pressured.

Sometimes, though, the situation changes of its own accord. I can think of a classic example of this when a known early-season hot-spot on the south bank of one of my favourite gravel-pits suddenly became decidedly 'cool'. For a couple of years 'in the know' spessy-types continued to set up in the swim a week or more before the start—but to no avail, the swim had died. I would like to think that the tench got fed-up with the regular early-season onslaught and moved on—but I doubt that such was the case, I suspect that the relocation of weedbeds was a far more significant factor.

What this sort of thing means in practical terms is that if you fish well-known tench waters it will soon become all too evident which are the productive swims—or at least, which are the popular swims. That is not to say that there will not be hitherto undiscovered hot-spots, but on hard-fished waters you cannot escape the crowds because if you are fortunate enough to discover a new swim, and do well there, it will simply join the list of popular swims for which everyone competes—as I have frequently found to my cost. It has always been in my nature to 'do my own thing' but whenever I have discovered new feeding areas, or even new waters, I have had to live with the fact that the situation can only be temporary because it will inevitably be sabotaged. Take the example of the lovely little swim I discovered on one of my favourite tench waters—it was in an otherwise unfancied area but early-season produced some very big fish for me. It was fishable only from a tiny gap in the bushes but I deliberately refrained from making it more comfortable because I knew that such an action would make it more popular with other anglers. So cramped was my little swim that I christened it 'The Cubby Hole'. But the inevitable happened and it was enlarged to accommodate a bivouac. One of its tenants saw fit to drag out a lot of the marginal weed that was part of the reason of its appeal to tench. Then a bunch of youngsters fished there for a whole weekend—not content with hacking down yet more branches so they could get 3 umbrellas in line, they left an enormous amount of filth and litter as well as using the rear of the pitch as a lavatory.

God I hate anglers. Many of them anyway.

I was so distressed that I did not fish the swim again for nearly 2 seasons—I did not even dare go back to look at the swim for to have done so would have resulted in my feeling positively homicidal towards

Sunrise in one of my favourite swims. Shortly after this picture was taken I took a seven plus.

some of the morons with whom we are compelled to share our waters.

So, unless you are particularly thick-skinned and are capable of living with this sort of thing (in which case you are reading the wrong book), I suggest you look to a neglected, relatively unfished water and try to find your own private piece of heaven.

If you find such a water (and, as discussed in the 'Big Tench' chapter, there are plenty about), I would recommend that you try to spend some time watching at the tail-end of the close-season. These sessions could, if rules permitted, be combined with some quite extensive plumbing.

Areas where tench are seen in the close-season are usually a good bet during the opening weeks. In some waters, though, tench are reluctant to show themselves and we are thus compelled to try to locate them by logic.

I would first be drawn to shallow, weeded areas. These are likely to be spawning areas and, as spawning can be such a protracted affair with lots of fits and starts in response to varying water temperatures, there are likely to be tench in such areas certainly until the back-end of July, sometimes well into August. What you may find, though, is that such areas show a diminishing number of big females as the weeks pass, while the smaller males will remain. This, I suspect, is the result of females leaving the spawning areas when their spawn has been shed—the males, on the other hand, seem reluctant to leave all the time there are a few spawn-laden females present. It seems that a mere handful of females can encourage quite a lot of males to remain in an area . . . sounds familiar!

In practical terms this means that early season hot-spots can remain productive for quite a long time, but opportunities for large specimens decline steadily. But when such spots 'die', they do so very suddenly— when the last of the ripe females leaves the area, most of the males depart too. So practically overnight a productive early-season swim can become virtually tench-less.

Spawning grounds apart, I look for features—shelves, humps and bars. It never fails to astonish me how much attraction a comparatively small feature can hold for a relatively large number of tench. Given a large area of more-or-less even-depth water in which is located a hump the size of, say, a dining-room table, I would expect that hump to have a number of tench permanently in residence.

Shelves (areas of depth change) have considerable attraction too. As do the margins of islands—and, of course, the margins of the main-bank itself.

You will find tench beneath various sorts of overhanging trees and bushes—also cover in the form of lilies and other floating-leaved plants. Emergent weeds, like rushes, have an attraction to them—as do ordinary rooted bottom weeds, particularly milfoil.

Normally I would look for a swim that provided a combination of factors—weeded margins beneath overhanging willows, for example, or a weed-covered sub-surface hump.

So far I have made no mention of weather as regards tench location. This is because I do not believe it influences *where* they feed (as it does with carp, for example), but it most certainly influences *how* they will feed.

Let me explain.

Tench do not respond to wind by moving down to the end of the lake towards which it is blowing—but they are likely to feed best in a swim that lies either at the down-wind end of the pit or, alternatively, is affected by a cross-wind.

Look at the diagram (Fig. 4). I have indicated the positions of four good tench pitches in an imaginary water—with amazing originality I have numbered the pitches 1 to 4! I considered calling them A, B, C and D, but decided against using all my best ideas in one book!

All 4 pitches will have resident fish, but all 4 pitches are most unlikely to fish equally well on any given day. If, for example, a nice warm southerly was blowing I would opt for either swim number 1 or swim number 2. I would only be happy with swims 3 and 4 if they were affected by a cross-wind, but if they were sheltered and therefore calm, I would not

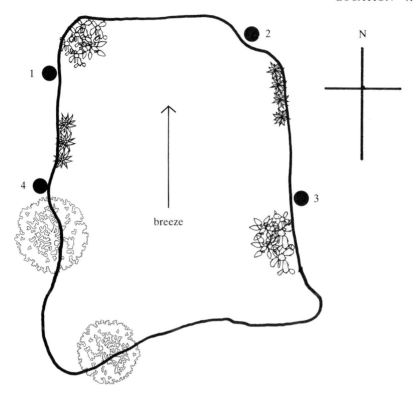

Fig. 4. Four holding swims on a pit—but their relative worth might be influenced by the breeze.

rate them very highly at all, but I would rate them higher than swims not identified as territorial holding-areas. In other words, top of the location priorities is the territorial or residential influence. Once I had identified good swims I would fish any one of them in preference to other swims on the water, even if other swims seemed to be more ideally located as regards wind direction. Ideally though, I would try to choose a swim that embodied the combined characteristics of tench preference and wind influence.

Most of the waters from which I catch my tench are heavily weeded— and great emphasis has been given by some writers to the benefits of weed-dragging. I disagree—very strongly actually. A bit of subtle weed clearance will do no harm, but over zealous weed removal will simply result in tench leaving the area. My policy is to try to find clear spots in the weed. This is usually quite easy early in the season but gets progressively more difficult as the weeks pass and the weed spreads, which causes the clear spots to shrink. Fortunately, so much of my tench fishing is close-in margin work that casting to even quite small clear spots is rarely very difficult. But difficult or not, it is worth locating areas of clear bottom in each of your selected swims—then by a combination of far-bank marks, reflections (in calm water) and casting 'feel', it is usually possible to cast to these with a high degree of consistency. That mention of casting 'feel' needs explaining—it is a sort of personal scale that goes something like this:

> underarm mini-swing
> underarm medium-swing
> underarm maxi-swing
> overarm gentle 'lob'
> overarm medium 'lob'
> ... and so on.

I also use other guides, like how far I can catapult hempseed, how far I can catapult maples etc. My distance guides, once established, are noted along with far-bank markers etc on a swim-plan. I can then move into any one of my repertoire of swims and place my baits exactly where I want to place them without having to disturb the swim by plumbing or test-casting.

At the conclusion of every session I plumb and test-cast to update my swim-plan and establish how the weed is encroaching on the clear spots. I may also go to a new, as yet untried swim, and test it out. It is therefore a process of constant monitoring rather than a case of making a swim-plan and relying on that plan for the rest of the summer. Swims change, sometimes dramatically, so regular updates are therefore essential.

Possibly I have made it sound like hard work, but in reality it is very simple because I will only be fishing a small number of swims and the monitoring is merely a matter of 10 minutes or so at the conclusion of each session.

My references to weed thus far have been to rooted weed such as milfoil and elodea, but an increasingly common trend in recent years has been that pits are becoming affected with filamentous weed like silk-weed or blanket weed. I hate the stuff and can recall catching very few tench over a bottom thus affected—one was my first 8-pounder but, despite the encouragement provided by that fish, few others followed it. I have tried neutral-density baits that sat nicely on top of the weed (it was one such that produced the 8 pounder) and pop-ups above it—but results to both approaches have been poor. I have come to the conclusion that it is far better to find a clear spot, no matter how small, rather than try to fish over silkweed or blanket weed. In the swim shown in the diagram (Fig. 5), for example, I would endeavour to put my baits in

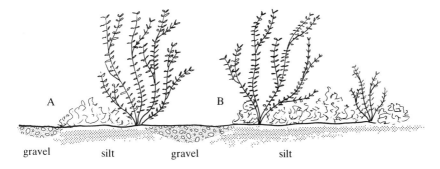

gravel   silt   gravel   silt

Fig. 5. Clear spots A and B are good spots—in this case the fact that they have
a gravel bottom makes them even better.

spots A and B. If there were no such clear spots I would find a nearby swim in which there were because this, in my experience, would be a much better bet than either fishing over the weed or trying to remove the weed by dragging.

Given the choice I would fish over sand or gravel in preference to mud. I remember as a youngster reading various references to tench being mud-lovers. I do not argue that tench can be caught in muddy-bottomed swims, but there is no doubt in my mind that sand and gravel are better.

The one other influence I would like to expand upon is that of depth. I have already said that shallow, weedy swims are likely to be best during the early part of the season, and indeed there will be a fair number of tench in such swims well into August, but that is not to say that shallow water has any intrinsic appeal when seen as a factor in isolation. Tench literature suggests that they are essentially shallow-water fish, and it will doubtless surprise many readers when I say that this is not so. Once the females have spawned they usually leave the spawning grounds and, if such are available, will drop down to deeper water. Most of my big tench have come from swims in excess of 17 ft deep; many have been caught in swims deeper than 20 ft. And do not for one moment imagine that my tench have been one-water-wonders! I have caught 7 lb plus tench from 5 different pits, in 4 of those 5 waters there are extensive areas of shallows as well as extensive areas of deeps—so the movement to deeper water demonstrates a preference on the part of the tench. So there is no need to be reluctant to fish deep water, because tench are by no means reluctant to feed in such spots!

You will notice that I have made no mention of pre-baiting. I would not have mentioned it in this section at all but as I have read so many references to the *creation* of tench swims by regular pre-baiting, I felt obliged to say something about it whilst discussing location.

Whether or not pre-baiting works in heavily stocked waters, I do not know. I have no interest in pulling out vast bags of medium sized tench so do not do that sort of fishing. In the relatively sparsely-stocked waters in which I do my fishing I am convinced that it has very little value. It might make a good swim better, but it will not persuade tench to visit a swim or feed in a swim that they would not otherwise have chosen. I have seen anglers who, unable to get the 'going swim', have absolutely piled the groundbait in a nearby swim in the hope of drawing tench into it—and it has not worked, no matter if they have sat there for a day or a week. Sometimes there are what appear to be encouraging signs such as rolling, but the fish obstinately refuse to get their heads down over the bait and feed.

I do, however, like to bait-up a swim the evening before a planned morning session because it enables me to start fishing without disturbing the swim. I do not worry too much if evening-baiting is not possible though—although I regard it as desirable, I do not think it is essential. In many waters the securing of a pitch is such an uncertain business anyway, that its worth is minimal—chances are you would merely be baiting-up for someone else's benefit.

So let me summarise:

1. If tench are seen cruising or rolling, there is likely to be a feeding area close by.
2. Early in the season, tench are likely to be in the vicinity of spawning grounds—these will probably be in shallow, weedy areas.
3. Features such as humps, bars and shelves are attractive to tench.
4. Rooted weeds such as milfoil and elodea are attractive to tench.
5. The margins of islands, and certain margin areas of the main bank, are likely to be good spots.
6. Overhanging trees and bushes may enhance the attraction of margin swims.
7. Reeds and lilies have an attraction to tench, and where present in the margins will enhance the attraction of those margins.
8. You cannot 'buy' tench with lots of groundbait—there is no substitute for good initial location.

Bait and Presentation

Worms

Worms are the most effective tench-bait by far, and so important are they to tench anglers that I shall discuss them in much more detail than might normally be expected.

I started by saying that worms are the best tench-bait, but not just any worm. To many anglers a worm is a worm is a worm ... but that is far from the truth.

So, down to details.

The best of them all is the gilt-tail worm. It looks very much like a redworm except for its tail, which is bright yellow. I get the impression that tench like the colour yellow and are attracted to it, or maybe it has a particular light-wave frequency to which tench are attuned—I don't know, but whatever the reason I have found that tench seem to respond to yellow baits, or baits with a bit of yellow in them, better than to any other colour. The conspicuous tail of the gilt-tail is, I am sure, part of the reason for its effectiveness.

The next best bait is a redworm. Redworms should not be confused with brandling worms, they may look superficially similar but the brandling is a very poor substitute.

To acquire redworms and gilt-tails you will need to breed your own or find a suitably-stocked compost-heap. You cannot buy them from tackle-shops, at least I have never seen them for sale—although I have often seen tubs of brandlings that have been incorrectly sold as redworms.

Fortunately it is a simple enough matter to establish a wormery, and once established the stock is self-perpetuating and requires very little looking after.

I like the free-standing sort of wormery rather than the sunk-in-the-ground sort; and any large container will suffice providing it can offer suitable drainage so the contents do not become waterlogged. An old water-butt, water header-tank or what-have-you will do, but I invested in a garden-centre type compost-bin and although it meant an initial outlay of about £15 it has had many years use.

First you need a starter-stock of worms (I shall come to that presently) and a good supply of rotting vegetable matter. Ordinary kitchen waste such as cabbage leaves, potato peelings and apple cores are good—but avoid milk or animal products or the wormery will smell and the worms might die. Be very wary of garden-waste, especially grass cuttings. The occasional light sprinkling of grass cuttings will benefit the wormery, but never dump a large amount in there or the wormery will overheat which will result in brandlings predominating.

The best material of all is the soiled straw, complete with droppings, from a rabbit hutch. My sons have now grown up and their rabbits have long since died, but for many years Snowy and Chestnut contributed hugely to the welfare of my worm stocks!

The reason that straw is so good is that it does not compact into a solid mass and thus keeps the compost relatively cool—and as intimated earlier, temperature is a key factor and controls what sort of worms will predominate. My experience convinces me that redworms and gilt-tails thrive in cooler conditions than do brandlings.

My sons used to line their rabbit-hutch with newspaper, inevitably that became damp and soiled whilst in the hutch and that was put in the wormery too. I discovered that redworms loved corrugated cardboard and would crawl inside the 'tubes' created by the corrugations—so it is worth tearing up the occasional cardboard box and putting that in.

Once established, the worms will breed prolifically and, short of disaster like a drought or severe frost, will be readily available all through the year. The only care that needs be heaped upon the heap (!) is to ensure that it remains damp and is kept topped-up with suitable waste vegetable matter.

Do not, incidentally, use any of the commercial compost-making preparations that are designed to speed-up the rotting process—they are fine for gardeners who merely want to dump the compost on their floribundi, or whatever they do with it, but they will inhibit worms.

If you do not have a garden you can use smaller containers such as buckets or, better still, fertiliser sacks—these have the advantage that they can be kept in a shed or garage and are thus protected from frost and excessive heat.

These small containers are not really suitable for kitchen waste, rabbit straw and the like because they do not hold the necessary volume of material to enable it to compact in the way it needs to if compost is to be formed. There is a fine balance, you see—there needs to be a degree of compaction, but not too much.

Small wormeries are best filled with the compost in which the worms are found—which brings me, as promised, to the business of obtaining a starter stock.

If you know a keen gardener who has a long-established compost-

Particles are effective both as feed and as hook-bait.

heap in his or her garden, the heap may hold a stock of worms—it depends whether or not compost-making chemicals have been used on the heap. But the best sources are farm muck-heaps, especially those on which stable or pig waste is dumped. If you can persuade a pig-farmer to allow you to dig in his muck-heap you will, I promise you, find worm-stocks beyond the dreams of avarice! Dig near the edge of the heap for redworms and gilt-tails (the edge of the heap being cooler than further in) because the further from the edge you go, the greater the proportion of brandlings you will find.

Take as much of the compost as you can carry—after all, they lived in the stuff right up to the moment you dug them out, so obviously it is an ideal environment for them.

You will find that mini-wormeries do not self-perpetuate quite so readily as do the larger versions, so I like to have 3 or 4 on the go and use them in rotation. When one container becomes somewhat depleted through use I leave it and move onto the next container. By the time I have returned to my original bag/bucket (probably several weeks later) the stock will have become re-established—well, partially so, but they are never as numerous as at the beginning.

The only attention these mini-wormeries require is an occasional helping of porridge (made only with water—no milk). I am being serious—they love it!

Bags can be tied-up and buckets may be fitted with a lid—but ensure that there are a few air-holes and that the air-holes remain clear.

You will notice that I have constantly referred to redworms and gilt-tails together, this is because I have not yet discovered how to acquire or breed gilts selectively. Among any stock of redworms will be a small percentage of gilt-tails; there are rarely many but I can usually find just enough for hookbait.

Brandlings, as I have said, are a very poor alternative. Tench will take them, but not with any enthusiasm. The occasional brandlings that turn up among my reds and gilts usually get thrown in with the ground-bait—or thrown on the lawn for the birds. I cannot imagine being desperate enough to put one on a hook—yes, I think they are *that* useless.

Some brandlings can be deceptively red in colour which can result in many anglers confusing them with redworms, but the giveaway is the yellow bands encircling the body—these are much wider and more obvious on a brandling than on a redworm. And even the reddest of brandlings cannot match the bright red of redworms.

Just occasionally I come across one that has me puzzled as to its identity—they look just like you would expect a redworm-brandling hybrid to look. Whether or not they can hybridise I do not know—but I do not worry too much about it because tench find these 'redlings', as I call them, quite acceptable.

I hook redworms and gilt-tails head-end only (Fig. 6). This is far superior to the normal practice of hooking them through the middle. Do not worry about missing bites—you will not, providing the hook is small and light enough, and providing the hook-link is relatively fine. For large redworms ('large' being relative because even the biggest of them are only about 7 or 8 centimetres long) I use a size 12 hook and a 4 pound test hook-link; while for the runts of the worm-world the hook needs to be reduced to a size 14 and the link should not be more than 3 pound test.

Both redworms and gilt-tails are relatively delicate baits and whilst head-hooking is far more secure than side-hooking they will not withstand anything more than medium-force casting. In practical terms it means that they are fine for distances up to, say, 30 metres or so, and can with care be cast up to about 50 metres, but they are not suitable for anything beyond. They are at their toughest when they are fresh from the wormery so although they will live for weeks in a bait-container (providing they do not become overheated) I do not recommend that they be kept in

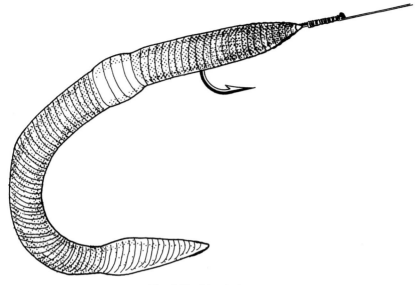

Fig. 6. Head-hooked worm.

this manner because they become rather fragile. Baits that have been kept in a bait container for a long while will only withstand the gentlest of casts. Their condition deteriorates, I imagine, when they do not have access to extensive food supplies.

If you want to cast a worm-bait a long way, forget all about redworms and gilt-tails and use lobworms.

Lobworms (or lawnworms, as they are sometimes called) can be collected from lawns after dark, especially if the ground is damp after rain. A calm night is best—they do not like wind.

You need to tread softly and, when a worm is seen in the torchlight, you try to ascertain which end is nearest the hole. This is not always easy to establish in grass—especially on anglers' lawns because, if they are anything like me, they would much rather go fishing than use a mower!

Having established which end is in the hole, you trap the worm with a finger—this should be done as near to the hole as possible. With your free hand (you will have to put the torch down or you will have insufficient hands!) you take hold of the worm and pull gently. It will by now have got a firm grip inside its hole and will have to be teased out very carefully—if you pull too hard it will break. I have found that a sort of Yuri Geller spoon-bending finger-and-thumb movement near the point where the tail of the worm disappears can encourage it to release its hold.

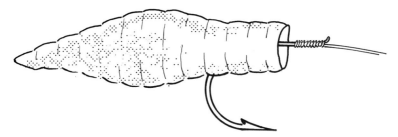

Fig. 7. Lob-tail for long casting.

As confidence and experience develops you may care to try a more advanced technique. Having 'snitched' (that is the technical expression) many thousands of worms I count myself, in all humility, as a bit of an expert in this technique—it is called the grab-and-snatch. If the worm is grabbed and pulled in one smooth, swift movement it can be plucked from its hole before it has a chance to get a grip (it grips by using thousands of body-bristles as anchors . . . be honest, how many of you knew that?).

Obviously a few worms break, but most are removed intact and, important this, unstretched. Stretched worms soon die, so the better condition they are in, the longer they last.

Even the most superbly conditioned lobworms will not keep for long though. The best medium in which to keep them consists of rough clods of broken turf—and they must be kept cool (in a 'fridge if possible). It is important to check them daily and remove any that are dead or dying . . . but in all honesty, it is so much hassle that I do not think it is worth it because no matter how much care you take, you cannot keep more than a few dozen. I therefore try to catch them as I need them—and never try to keep them for more than a few days. If weather conditions are such that I cannot obtain a supply—I do without and use something else.

If you look at a lobworm you will see that it has a dark, pointed, purple-ish end. That's the head. And a flattish, paler end . . . go on, have a guess! (In case any jet-skiers or wind-surfers are having this read aloud to them, I'll save them the agonies of intellectual effort and tell them that's the tail!)

The tail-end is the bit that we use for bait.

A 4 or 5 centimetre length of lob-tail on a size 10 or 8 hook (Fig. 7) can be cast as far as you could possibly want. It is a very tough bait indeed. And whilst I would not claim that it is in quite the same league as a gilt-tail or redworm, it is nonetheless a very good bait and one that I use with complete confidence.

There are other worms but to be honest I have too little experience

of them to offer worthwhile opinions as to their effectiveness—my 'favourite 3' are so good that I have not felt the need to experiment with others.
I have used those white-ish, very tough worms that can be dug from
the garden, the sort that curl up into a tight ball when removed from
the soil, but I cannot actually recall catching a tench on one. I have
caught a few tench on those pinky-white worms that you find in leaf-
mould, but insufficient to inspire me to deliberately seek them out. Those
blue-ish worms that can be dug from marshy ground (marsh-worms, presumably), have, in my limited use of them, proved to be quite effective—
and not just for tench, I have caught carp and bream on them too. And
eels, but that is no recommendation—eels will eat anything (I only put
that in to raise the hackles of the eel-boys, they hate it when the foul,
slimy things are denigrated!).

But talk of other worms is purely academic—as far as I am concerned
there are only 3 varieties: gilts, reds and lobs. And if there is a God,
he wasted a perfectly good chunk of the 6 days of creation by creating
any others—he would have been far better employed dotting the weald
of Kent with a vast network of interconnecting gravel-pits . . .

Maggots

Tench undoubtedly like maggots, but I rate them better as feed than
as hookbait. Their disadvantage is that being so small, they can only
properly be presented on a very small hook in conjunction with an ultra-
light link. And frankly, I cannot think of one tench water where such
a combination would be appropriate. Some anglers may argue that we
can get round the presentation-problem by using bunches of maggots,
perhaps by threading a dozen or so on a silk 'hair' and wrapping that
'hair' round the hook. Such approaches may or may not work, certainly
I have read of instances where anglers claim to have done well with the
technique, but it has never worked well for me.

So I use maggots as feed—and in that role they are superb. My
favourite maggots are squatts which, because they are so small and slug-
gish, can be crammed in a groundbait-ball without causing it to break
up. If I tell you that there are about 6,000 squatts to the pint (compared
with about 2,000 hook-maggots to the pint) you can imagine just how
many tiny feed-items it is possible to cram into 3 or 4 tangerine-size
groundbait balls. Squatts, therefore, enable us to create the illusion of
there being a lot of food in the pitch, without running the risk of the
tench feeding to satiation.

Ordinary maggots are good too but because they are so active cannot
be so tightly packed into the groundbait-ball. The fact that they are so
active also means that they deteriorate rapidly if they are not properly
looked after. Most anglers take their bait-container into a tackle shop,

buy the required quantity of maggots, and give them no further thought until they are required for use, which may be 2 or 3 days later—by which time they are stinking of ammonia and as tough as old boots.

Until required for use, maggots should be kept in a wide, shallow container (I have a couple of washing-up bowls that I bought for the purpose)—and ideally they should be riddled daily and placed in fresh bran after each riddling. This ensures that the maggots stay clean and sweet—and far superior to those used by most anglers.

The only feed items that are superior to maggots are casters. Few specialist or specimen anglers realise just how effective a feed item casters are. Matchmen have recognised the worth of casters for a long while, but specialist anglers have been slow to capitalise on that knowledge. I would go so far as to say that I do not know of anything that can be used for mass feed that matches the effectiveness of casters. They are *that* good. They are also an absolute pain to produce in sufficient quantity—and the timing has to be spot-on. Matchmen will sit up all night riddling, packing and refrigerating casters as soon as they turn—and whilst I do not doubt the worth of what they do, and whilst I am lost in admiration at the level of their dedication, I just do not have that level of application. So I take an easier route. Now, whilst I do not for one moment claim that the casters I produce are in the same league as those produced by matchmen, they are attractive feed-items for tench. You will need to go to a tackle dealer who sells 'caster maggots'—these are not a special breed, they are simply maggots that have had their development held back by refrigeration. If they are bought during the afternoon of the day preceding a tench session, and kept overnight in ordinary garage/boot-of-the-car temperature, the bulk of them will turn overnight. Those that have not turned will do so during the course of the morning's fishing. The early-turners will, by the time they are used, have become floaters. That does not matter—there is no need to separate them because they will simply float away and become duck-food. The matchmen cannot afford to have this happen or it may encourage fish to rise in the water and follow wind or current borne floaters out of his swim. Tench are most unlikely to rise up in the water so the problem does not arise.

Casters produced this way are smaller than those produced from maggots that have not been held back, they are tougher too—but in a tench fishing context they are highly effective.

Casters, of course, do not wriggle—a lot of them can therefore be crammed in a groundbait ball. According to Ivan Marks (from whom I got my other figures), there are about 3,000 casters to the pint—so for a given number of groundbait balls you will only have about half as many casters in the swim as you would squatts—but that still represents an awful lot of feed items, and what is more they are feed items that tench absolutely love.

If you read match fishing literature you will come across 'special' maggots such as sour-brans and gozzers. I have bred and used these specials and endorse their effectiveness as hookbaits, especially for bream, but as stated earlier, I do not think maggots have much relevance as hookbaits in most tench waters—and as it is neither practical nor necessary to try to use 'specials' as feed items I do not think there would be any useful purpose served by my describing how to produce them. It would be impossible to produce them in sufficient quantity anyway.

Seeds, Beans and Pulses

I always include hempseed in my tench feed because I have tremendous confidence in its ability to hold fish in a pitch. But here we have something of a puzzle—I have *never* found regurgitated hempseed in a keepsack after it has held a tench. I have found bread, crushed boilies, bits of corn etc, but never hempseed. So although I am convinced that tench eat hempseed, I do not know for certain that they do. But I have so much faith in it that nothing would persuade me to omit it from my feed—and I am a great believer in the 'Why change a winning team?' adage anyway.

Usually I mix my hempseed 50/50 with tares and cook great batches of it in a massive pasta-pot. After cooking it is packed in half-kilo (approximately one pound) packs and stored in my bait-freezer until I require it. Some anglers believe that fresh-cooked hempseed is superior to frozen hempseed—they may be correct but I have never been able to detect any difference.

I do not pre-soak my hemp (or tares)—I simply half fill a pan with seeds, top up with water, bring it to the boil and simmer between 25 and 35 minutes (until a little white shoot appears from the hempseed).

It is then allowed to cool in the water in which it was cooked—after which it is transferred to a mesh-bag (like the jelly-bag used by home wine-makers) and hung in the garden to drain.

If you are in a hurry you can cool cooked hempseed by dousing it in cold water—but on no account try this with tares or they will split.

My Belgian friends, who are the ultimate specialists with hempseed (it was the Belgians who first introduced hempseed fishing into the UK) tell me that the seeds should be pre-soaked before cooking. This, evidently, allows the seeds to germinate. I respect their advice, but I have been led to believe that the hempseed sold in this country is treated (irradiated, perhaps?) to prevent it germinating—presumably to ensure that UK gardens are not filled with 'Grow-Bags' bursting with thriving clumps of marijuana!

Maple peas are a good tench bait and are large enough to be used on the hook as well as for feed. Due, I imagine, to their dark colour (when cooked they are almost black) they do not have instant appeal, but once tench acquire a taste for them they are very effective indeed. I know waters where carp anglers were forced to quit using maples because tench took them so enthusiastically.

Tench love chick-peas too, and unlike maples they are a highly visible bait that have a nice yellow colour when cooked (and, if you recall, I said earlier that tench seem to be attracted to yellow baits). Chick-peas also take flavours and sweetener very readily, so it is possible to incorporate any of the usual boilie-flavours. I have done well with caramel flavoured chick-peas that have been sweetened and had their natural yellow colour boosted with a few drops of yellow food-dye. I recommend that you use flavours and sweeteners at about half the stated rate for boilies. If, for example, you are using a flavour that is recommended for use at 5 ml to the pound of boilie-mix, use 2½ ml to the pound (dry, uncooked weight) of chick-peas. The flavour, sweetener and dye are added to the water at the initial soaking stage and cooked in the same water.

Do not try to flavour or sweeten maple peas, incidentally, they are almost completely resistant—they have a strong, attractive flavour of their own anyway.

After an overnight (or 12 hour) soak, maples and chick-peas are brought to the boil and simmered for about 20 minutes (up to 30 minutes in the case of chick-peas if you want a slightly softer bait), drained and allowed to cool.

Good as maples and chick-peas are, the particle bait on which I have caught most tench is the 'magic' black-eyed bean. Len Burgess and I were introduced to these by Rod Hutchinson in the days before he became a tackle-tycoon and international media-star! In those days he fished with tackle that had to be seen to be believed (or heard—his reels sounded like nuts and bolts being stirred in a galvanised bucket!)—and talk about ill-equipped, he once crept up behind a friend late in the evening and said, 'Have you got a hook I could have? I've lost my spare one.'

I kid you not!

Anyway, in those high and far off days, despite appalling tackle, he still managed to show us a thing or 2 about catching carp—and as I said, he introduced Len and me to black-eyes. Knowledge of particle fishing a year or 2 in advance of its widespread use enabled us to do well on some waters from which we had hitherto been unsuccessful—and I discovered, as many have done since, that the appeal of black-eyes was not confined to carp. Armed with 'Susies' (code-name for black-eyes ... 'Oh my pretty little black-eyed Susie ...') I proceeded to catch tench that, for those days, were very big fish indeed. I recall catching my first ever 6-pounder on black-eyes, and following it up with one of 5 lb 15 oz—thus missing a brace of sixes by the narrowest of margins. Alright, so nowadays a brace of sixes would rank as a good catch, even a very good catch, but by national standards would not be considered exceptional. In those days, however, it was the sort of catch that produced wide-eyed amazement, not to say disbelief, among tench specialists. Most tench anglers had never even seen a 6-pounder, let alone come within a barbule of catching 2 in a morning! 'Fives' were the target-fish in those days—and in truth, they were difficult enough to come by ... mention of which reminds me that even earlier than the 'Susie era', circa 1970 or thereabouts, I once caught 3 tench over 5 lb in one July afternoon. I photographed the fish individually (as they were caught) and returned them to the water immediately after photographing, so I did not have a photograph of the 3 fish together—and I recall that there was undisguised disbelief in the eyes of some tench specialists when I told them about the catch—3 over 5 lb in a *season* would have afforded star-status in those days!

Only those of us who have been tench fishing since the 60's and 70's (and in my case, the 50's) can appreciate just how dramatically it has changed.

Back to black-eyes.

I experimented with several dyes and flavours because, like chick-peas, they take dyes and flavours readily, but I concluded that Rod's original method was best. He recommended that the beans be cooked (after pre-soaking) in a really thick tomato soup (made by using at least twice the stated quantity of tomato soup powder—or half the quantity of water ... depends how you look at it!) for 20 minutes, then allowed to cook in the soup. Rod liked to use the beans with as much congealed, soupy 'gunge' attached to them as possible ... after catapulting them out in this state, particularly against a facing wind, you became so spattered with soup that it looked as though you'd been in a road accident!

A particle that requires no preparation at all is sweetcorn—and many tench anglers would argue that this is the most effective particle of them all. Certainly it is a very good bait—it is bright in colour (*that* colour, again) and very sweet-tasting. There is no doubt that tench love it.

The fact that it is so readily available and so convenient to use has led to it being over-used in some waters which, in turn, has led to tench becoming wary of it. But in waters where it has not been over-used or, rather more likely, where it was once used to excess but has now fallen into disuse, it can be superb.

I recommend that you buy the best sweetcorn (Jolly Green Giant being my choice) because cheaper brands contain smaller kernels and lots of unusable 'bits'.

Corn can be used as both feed and hook-bait, and when used as hook-bait works well as a single grain on a small hook or anything up to half a dozen grains on a larger hook. When I first used corn (and other particles) I fished the grains directly on the hook—but with the advent of the hair I switched to the new presentation and was soon convinced that it was superior.

There are doubtless many other particles that will catch tench—well, I know there are, including one that I rate very highly but cannot reveal because it was disclosed to me in confidence—but rest assured that those I have mentioned are excellent baits and will catch a lot of tench.

Before leaving the subject of particles I will add as a post-script that the nuts beloved by carp anglers are not, in my experience, good tench baits. I have used peanuts and tiger nuts for carp in waters where there are plenty of tench and have only had a couple on peanuts and none at all on tigers.

I am told that tench take hazel nuts quite readily but I cannot confirm it with personal experience because it is a bait that I have hardly ever used—it would not surprise me though, because cooked hazel nuts are quite soft, and as a generalisation I would say that tench prefer softer baits than do carp.

Pastes

Pastes made from tinned pet-foods like Kit-e-Kat are good tench baits. To make a pet-food paste you empty the contents of a tin into a bowl, mash it to crush any hard bits, and then mix with a 50/50 mix of Weetabix and semolina until a nice firm paste is obtained. I always used to add a level teaspoonful of salt to the mixture because salt toughens the gluten found in the binder which, in turn, made the paste more elastic.

Sausage-meat paste is another good bait and is made in exactly the same way described for pet-food paste.

But the very best paste bait I have ever used was made from salmon fry crumb. It is like a superior quality trout pellet and the variety I used was obtained from BP Nutrition based at Witham in Essex. To buy direct, which is by far the most economical way of obtaining it, you have to buy a minimum of 25 kilo. If you want smaller quantities you will have to buy it from carp-bait suppliers (and pay their mark-up of course).

Salmon crumb is very easy to prepare—it merely has to be dampened, left to stand for half an hour or so, then kneaded into a paste.

I caught very many tench on this bait back in the early 70's—in fact I think that the 3 fives in an afternoon that I mentioned earlier were probably taken on it.

I rarely use pastes these days, but when I do I no longer mould it round the hook as I used to—instead I tie a tiger nut or bead to the end of a hair and mould the paste around that (Fig. 8). A grape-size piece of paste on a size 8 is a good combination.

Alternatively the paste can be moulded round a mini poly-ball or

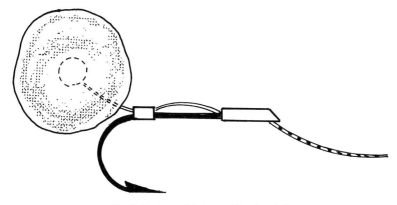

Fig. 8. Paste moulded round bead on hair.

piece of rig-foam and create a pop-up. Even as I write this I am wondering why I do not use this method more often because it is very effective.

Luncheon Meat

I have heard of some very good catches of tench on luncheon meat but have myself only taken a few fish on it. It would appear to be particularly useful for fishing over silt where, due to its high fat content and consequent buoyancy, it settles lightly on the softest bottom.

Bread

From 1980 to 1982 I logged all the big-tench reports that appeared in the angling Press and found to my surprise that the bait that accounted for the most fish was bread (you can read the full results of the survey in 'Modern Specimen Hunting'). I accept that in a rough-and-ready survey based, as it was, on Press reports (some of which are extremely questionable) and with no proper controls applying, it can be misleading to read too much into resulting statistics. I accept, too, that the fact that bread came out top in the survey does not mean that bread is the best bait—after all, the survey took no account of the frequency with which the various baits were used. But even with such reservations in mind I would caution against dismissing too readily the effectiveness of bread as a big tench bait. My experience suggests that for tench (and bream too, incidentally) it is a very good bait—no, I would not expect it to come out top, but certainly I would rank it very highly.

Although I have used it occasionally as a paste and frequently as flake, the form in which I have used it most often is as pressed crust.

To make pressed crust you require a 3-day old white tin loaf. Crusts are removed from the loaf with about 12 mm (half an inch) of crumb attached. A slab of crust is placed on a damp tea-towel, another damp tea-towel is placed on top, a bread-board or similar is placed on top of that, and weights (heavy mail-order catalogues are ideal) are placed on top of the board. It is then left overnight.

On being removed from the press, the crust will be compressed and quite firm and, unlike unpressed crust, it will sink.

To keep it in good condition while fishing I keep ready-cut cubes in an airtight sandwich box, along with a couple of thick slices of raw potato to prevent drying-out.

The cubes can be mounted directly on a size 10 hook or, as I prefer, hair-rigged on a size 12.

Boilies

Recent seasons have seen a dramatic change in tench fishing tactics in that boilies are now very widely used for the species. This situation came about because in many waters tench have developed a taste for boilies having encountered their use by carp anglers. This has led to tench anglers developing the approach for themselves.

I find the 14 mm size the most useful, although I have caught plenty on 16 mm baits. Tench will take 18 mm baits, and larger, but I do not recommend them because very rarely will they prove to be as effective as smaller versions.

Mini-boilies in the 8 to 10 mm range are popular with some tench anglers but I rarely use them for hook-bait, I do use them as loose-feed though. Cubed particle boilies of 10 mm or so are another matter—I use them a lot. I shall discuss those presently when I talk about making boilies.

A lot of big tench are caught on commercial ready-mades, but I never use them (except, as mentioned in the previous paragraph, the frozen mini variety as loose-feed). If I were to use ready-mades I think I would use the frozen varieties in preference to shelf-life ones because I do not know what preservatives are used in shelf-life baits. I would be much happier if the manufacturers gave details of what preservatives their baits contained so we would know whether or not they were preservatives that were permitted for human consumption. I would like to know how much preservative goes in as well. I am not suggesting that currently available shelf-life baits are harmful to fish, but I adopt a general guiding principle with boilies that I would not include anything that I would not be prepared to eat myself—nor would I use anything at any level that I would not be prepared to eat myself. I cannot apply that principle to shelf-life baits because the manufacturers do not tell us what is in

Boilie-making.

them. I suspect that potassium sorbate is used and, providing it is used at low levels, I have no worries about this preservative. When I use potassium sorbate to slow deterioration in long-session baits, I use it at the rate of 1 gm of preservative to 1000 gm of base-mix (this being the rate recommended to me by a food technologist).

So, bait manufacturers—over to you. Are you prepared to identify what preservatives you use? And at what levels?

There is no doubt that tench find ready-mades highly palatable—doubtless due in part to the fact that most of them are very sweet; in fact shelf-life ready-mades have a very high sugar content (which is why they go sticky). The high sugar level, incidentally, is probably used as much for its role as a preservative as for its palliative qualities.

But my preference, as I have said before, is to make my own. And the most effective tench-boilie I have ever used is a fish-meal bait that employs some natural extracts instead of artificial flavours. It also includes a protein-digest which, I believe, releases amino acid attractants that amplify the nutritional signal and evoke a feeding response.

It also employs high-quality milk proteins that provide a readily digestible food source.

There are doubtless cynics among you who are thinking that I will not reveal the bait I *really* use and will describe instead a second-best, also-ran. You are wrong. The bait I am about to describe is the best tench-boilie I have ever used—the response it evokes is the most dramatic I have ever experienced. So why am I writing about it? Why not keep it to myself? I considered doing just that!

On deliberation, though, I decided that the bait is just too much trouble for most anglers to undertake—so even a detailed recipe will not result in it being over-used.

I hope!

Here it is:

First I make a base-mix which consists of:

1 kilo spray-dried 100 mesh acid casein
1 kilo Irish 30 mesh acid casein
2 kilo Danish spray-dried calcium caseinate
1 kilo soya isolate (gel type)
500 gm Whey-pro
500 gm wheat gluten
500 gm albumen
1 kilo lactalbumin

This is thoroughly mixed and then stored in a cool, dry place and used as required for my carp and tench baits.

To 198 gm (7 oz) of the base-mix I add:

28 gm (1 oz) semolina
85 gm (3 oz) mixed fish-meal (details to follow)
7 ml Dutch shrimp additive
10 ml Lactamino
5 ml vitamin/mineral mix

All the named ingredients are mixed together by placing them in a strong poly-bag, blowing in the bag to inflate it, holding the neck of the bag tight and shaking thoroughly.

Five size 3 eggs are broken into a bowl and to them is added 10 ml of liquid seafood essence and 15 ml sesame seed oil. This is beaten until completely blended, then the dry ingredients are added.

First the mixture is stirred with a fork, then kneaded by hand. Finally the dough is rolled into 14 mm baits with a Gardner Rollaball bait-maker, and boiled in 170 gm (6 oz) batches for 45 seconds. They are allowed to dry and cool, then bagged-up and frozen.

I always put a little bit of the mixture aside and use it to make pop-ups. Some anglers grill or micro-wave their pop-ups, I prefer to use those tiny poly-balls that are sold as bean-bag filler. Three tiny poly-balls are right for a 14 mm boilie, I find.

This recipe, incidentally, has a protein level of about 60%. A lot of anglers miscalculate the protein level of their baits by including indigestible material such as gluten in the calculation.

That mixed fish-meal I mentioned is also made up as a bulk-mix, it consists of:

1 kilo white fish-meal
1 kilo anchovy and sardine meal
250 gm capelin meal
100 gm albumen

The extra albumen is added because with fish-meal forming about 30% of the mix there would not be quite enough albumen in the rest of the mix to do its job of binder effectively.

I buy my bait ingredients from Colne Valley Baits and from Specialist Bait Supplies (SBS). And no, I do not get them free—I pay the going rate and only qualify for the same reductions as anyone else, ie a small deduction for a bulk order.

Another recipe with which I have caught an enormous number of big tench is:

2 kilo mixed casein
2 kilo lactalbumen
1 kilo sodium caseinate
1 kilo calcium caseinate

1 kilo soya isolate
2 kilo semolina
500 gm gluten
250 gm albumen
250 gm vitamin/mineral mix
283 gm (10 oz) of this mixture are added to 6 size 3 eggs—then rolled
out and cooked as already described.

This bait has a protein level of about 60% and has worked well with both sweet and savoury flavours. The best sweet versions I have used have been with Maplecreme (Rod Hutchinson) and Caramel (Geoff Kemp) flavours—although, to be honest, I think most of the creamy, fruity flavours work well with tench. Sweeteners seem to improve the effectiveness of the bait yet further so I generally use 2 ml of liquid sweetener or 7 gm (¼ oz) of powder sweetener per 283 gm (10 oz) dry-mix.

'Savoury' flavours like lobster, meat and salmon work well too. I put 'savoury' in inverted commas because the flavours are made with combinations of chemicals which, except in the case of nature-identical flavours, bear no resemblance to their designated label. I generally use sweeteners with these too. One of the best savoury flavours for tench was discovered by my friend Bob Ball—it being Richworth's Savoury-Bacon. I think it is awful stuff—I kept my mini-bottle inside a larger screw-top plastic container and still it stank to high heaven ... but the tench loved it! Bob discovered how effective it was when he kept catching tench on savoury-bacon boilies from a water that normally produced hardly any.

But, in truth, tench are not overly fussy about flavours and they will take most things ... except garlic! They do not seem to like essential oil garlic, and one of my carp fishing friends uses this knowledge to try to make his carp-baits tench-proof. It seems to work—in some waters at least. As to the other essential oils, I do not know whether tench like them or not—I have neither the personal experience nor the feedback from friends on which I can base an opinion.

Do not confuse essential oils with bulk oils—tench seem quite partial to sesame seed oil, olive oil and fish oils like pilchard oil and cod liver oil. A very good tench bait additive that was recommended to me many years ago by Duncan Kay is Codlivene, which is a cod liver oil rich animal-feed supplement.

Tench feed differently from carp and we need to be cognizant of this fact when we consider how best to present our baits.

Tench are more inclined to hold hard baits in their lips and mouth, rather than pass them directly to the pharyngeals as carp often do. So we need to have the bait much closer to the hook than is the case with the standard carp hair-rig. Just how long the hair needs to be depends

Unhooking a big tench.

on the bait, but it only needs be sufficiently long to allow a 'hinge' of a couple of millimetres.

I have caught innumerable tench on single, bottom-fished boilies but my favourite presentation is with 2 boilies on a hair, comprising a pop-up counterbalanced by a sinker (Fig. 9).

Ordinary pop-ups are good too (Fig. 10)—tench seem to prefer their bait to stand proud or be off the bottom.

Single 14 mm pop-ups I fish on a size 8; double baits I fish on a size 6.

Before leaving the subject of boilies, I promised that I would mention particle boilies. These are simply cubed boilies (usually about 1 cm size) that are made from a boilie-mix by first rolling the mix into 1 cm thick slabs and putting those slabs in the freezer for a quarter of an hour or so—this firms them up. The slabs are then cubed with a sharp knife and cooked for 45 seconds as per ordinary boilies.

I often make particle boilies because:

(a) A lot of tench fishing is done at close-range, and at close-range there is no advantage in boilies being spherical—aerodynamic

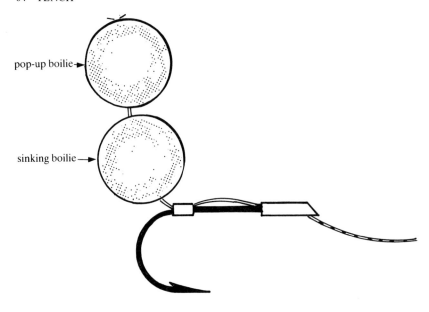

Fig. 9. Neutral-density combination bait.

qualities being unimportant.
(b) Particle boilies are incredibly easy to make; I can knock out
    Gillians (has it occurred to you that the girl's name, Gillian,
    sounds like a number ... millions, billions, trillions, Gillians ...?)
    of them in no time at all.

It goes without saying that (b) is a much stronger selling-point than
(a)!

Groundbait

A lot of my tench fishing, as I have said, is at very close range,
the margins and just beyond, so groundbaiting often need only comprise
loose-feed. My choice in that sort of situation is to feed the swim with
hempseed or a hemp/tare mixture, generally this will comprise about
226 gm (8 oz) cooked weight if the seeds go out that morning, or twice
that amount if they go out the evening before.

Also I like to put out a few pouches of a larger particle such as
maple peas or black-eyes.

In addition there will be a few hook-samples, not many, just half
a dozen or so round each hook-bait.

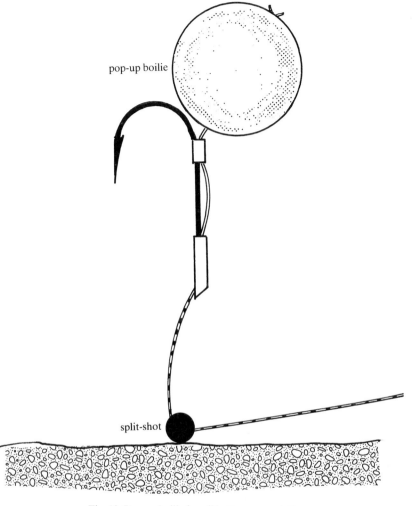

pop-up boilie

split-shot

Fig. 10. Pop-up boilie for off-bottom presentation.

The amounts described will go out before starting but no more will be put out until fish are caught—I will then top-up with 4 or 5 pouches of mixed feed after each fish.

As well as pre-feeding the swim I like to lace it with maggots or casters every 30 minutes or so. This must be done very quietly, while remaining out of sight. Where the range and absence of nuisance fish makes it practical to feed in this manner it offers a two-fold attraction: first, the visual element and, second, a vertical 'curtain' of detectable scent-trail food-signals through which tench may pass—and if they do I think it likely that they may be stimulated into looking for food which, in turn, may lead them to find and feed on groundbait. Alright, so it is theory! But I am convinced that there is merit in the idea.

Oil in or on baits might achieve the same effect via an ascending 'curtain' of mini-droplets.

The sort of mixed-bag that sometimes falls to worm—a 7 lb tench, a pike and a bream. A roach was added to the catch after these were returned!

Where the range is such that it is impossible to catapult loose-feed far enough, we either need to use a bait-dropper or use groundbait as a carrier. I use both methods, but generally prefer the groundbait because I believe it can be made attractive in its own right.

My groundbait consists of the following (the measures are by volume, incidentally, I usually use an old mug for the purpose):

6 measures of white crumb
2 measures of layer's mash

1 measure of roast barley that has been kibbled (ground up but left in bits, not reduced to a powder)

1 measure of fish-meal (I used to use ground-up trout pellets but find the fish-meal just as good and more convenient.)

All ingredients should be fresh and sweet-smelling.

This mixture holds together well for catapulting but on impact with the water breaks up into a lot of enticing particles that tench obviously find to their liking. A tangerine size ball is crammed with hempseed and maggots or casters; 2, 3 or sometimes 4 such balls are put out to each hook-bait position before starting fishing. No more groundbait is put out until a fish is caught—after which I will put out another 1 or 2 balls to the spot from which the fish was taken.

This same groundbait is used as a feeder-plug when I use semi open-ended feeders—but I shall talk more about that in the appropriate section.

Please remember — litter loses fishing

Methods and Tactics

The most efficient means of bite indication is a float, but for float fishing to give of its best the fishing conditions must fulfil certain criteria:

1. The range should be fairly close—say, up to 15 metres
2. The wind should be gentle—or better still, non-existent
3. There should be little or no sub-surface drag
4. The swim should be such that it is possible to use light line (approximately 4.5 lb maximum)

A good float angler will be able to fish in circumstances other than those described and may well argue with my upper-limit on line strength—but coping in other than ideal conditions involves compromise, and there comes a point when the degree of compromise is such that it is difficult to fish efficiently and it would probably make more sense to use another method.

From which you may conclude that I do not regard float fishing as a particularly useful method for tench—and you would be right. But to be fair, it has to be said that I do not particularly enjoy float fishing and so rarely employ it even when all my criteria are fulfilled. While writing this I have been trying to remember when I last caught tench on float tackle and, for the life of me, I cannot. I *have* caught tench by float fishing, but not many and certainly not recently. I make that admission because I do not want to pretend to be something I'm not—and I'm not a particularly good float angler.

So, to anyone who really wants to learn how to use float tackle efficiently I say, 'Read-up the matchmen'. Current match fishing literature is full of information relating to pole-fishing which, even if it were a practical proposition for tench, would not appeal to me in the slightest ... poles are awful things. I do not for one moment doubt their efficiency, but they are so big and clumsy—I could never enjoy using one. I recommend, therefore, that you visit your local library and try to get hold of some of the older books—one that taught me an awful lot (not just about float fishing, but legering too) was 'Ivan Marks on Match Fishing' by Ivan Marks and John Goodwin (Pelham). Another was 'World Class

Match Fishing' by Kevin Ashurst and Colin Dyson (Cassell). Both books were published in the mid-70's, but do not let that fact count against them—they are full of useful information. Another useful one, and a more recent publication, is David Hall's 'The Match Fisherman' (Pelham). If you are lucky you might come across a copy of 'Match Angling' which was edited by the late John Carding (Pan). If so, read and digest Dave Rossi's chapter on long-range float fishing in still and slow water—it is excellent.

The aforementioned books contain superb advice on bait preparation and the use of groundbait too—I guarantee your tench fishing will profit from reading them. Mine certainly did.*

What follows, then, should not be seen as a substitute for reading-up the experts, it should merely be looked upon as a get-you-by guide.

My choice of float would be a bodied-waggler that would carry the equivalent of a couple of AAA shot. I arrange the shot so there is a BB (or smaller) resting on the bottom—this is my anchor-shot—while the bulk-shot would be bunched about 5 or 6 feet higher. DAM or Duncan Kay float-stops are used to set the depth (I used to use stop-knots, but these float-stops are obviously superior).

After casting, the line between float and rod-top is sunk using a special line-sinking compound made to Dick Walker's recipe—it consists of a mud-ball made by mixing washing-up liquid and Fullers Earth (you can buy Fullers Earth in chemist shops) until a dough-like consistency is achieved. If the line is pulled through the mud-ball every so often, it will behave itself beautifully.

My first choice of bait would be a gilt-tail worm, which, as I intimated earlier, is the best tench bait in the universe, or a redworm, which is the second best. My hook would be a size 12—probably a Partridge Z2, or maybe a sproat-bend wet-fly hook. The Drennan feeder-hook is nice too.

If eels or small perch made the use of a worm impractical, I would use a small cube of compressed crust on a size 10 or 12. It would be a somewhat reluctant second choice though, because the gilt-tail and red-worm are without doubt far superior.

Maggots and casters are superb feed items but do not readily lend themselves to use as hook-bait for the simple reason that it is impossible to achieve good presentation with such small baits on the sort of tackle necessary to deal safely with big tench. Were it possible to fish safely with a size 18 hook and 1.7 lb line, then both maggots and casters would doubtless be excellent.

Seed baits are worth a try, as are various paste baits. Even mini-boilies have their uses. But there is no doubt at all in my mind that where circumstances permit the use of light tackle, you cannot beat a small worm.

* Two books in this series cover float fishing very thoroughly—see back cover for details.

Loading the feeder.

Feeder-Fishing

My favourite method of tench fishing is light-line feeder-fishing. It is only suitable where weed is sparse enough to permit the safe use of a hook-link of between 4 and 5 lb test. You *can* push the method to its limits and use 6 lb test—but the combination of such a heavy link and the correspondingly heavy-wire hook needed to balance it, will not allow the method to give of its best.

After experimenting with numerous feeder-tackles and rejecting them all because of their tendency to tangle, I concluded that only 2 are satisfactory. One was borrowed from matchmen and is a fixed-paternoster with a blood-knot providing the junction. I shall not describe it because it has since been superseded by another, more efficient version—but if you want to try the knot-junction paternoster you will find it described in my book 'Modern Specimen Hunting'.

The version I now use incorporates a revolving leger-bead; a diagram (Fig. 11) will explain the set-up clearer than will words.

If you want to experiment with running-paternoster arrangements incorporating swivels, beads and bits of boom-tube, I wish you well—but I warn you in advance, I have probably been there! I have seen many suggestions for so-called tangle-free feeder-rigs and honestly cannot believe that those who recommend them can possibly have used them for any length of time—I found that even the most limited use revealed their shortcomings. Particularly to be avoided are rigs that involve any sort of mini-boom because when the tackle twists in flight, as it assuredly will, any attempt to straighten it (retrieving, for example) causes the twists to bunch-up to the boom and then lock in position. They do this because the boom becomes the base of a rigid triangle. Do not take my word for it—try it and see. Actually that is a good piece of advice—about not taking my word for it, I mean. I earnestly recommend that you take nothing as true, whether written by me or anyone else, until you have proved it for yourself.

The most important element of my rig, apart from its tangle-free properties, is the length of the hook-link. So often we read about tench giving mini-bites—and that has persuaded some anglers to use shorter and shorter hook-lengths, sometimes as short as an inch or two, in conjunction with ultra-sensitive means of registering mini-bites. This combination is seen as a solution to the problem.

It is not.

Such approaches actually exacerbate the problem.

Instead, I recommend that you use a long hook-link (4 feet is a good starting point) which, used in conjunction with a small, relatively lightweight hook, will result in lovely sailaway bites.

If twitches still occur, I recommend that you lengthen the hook-link

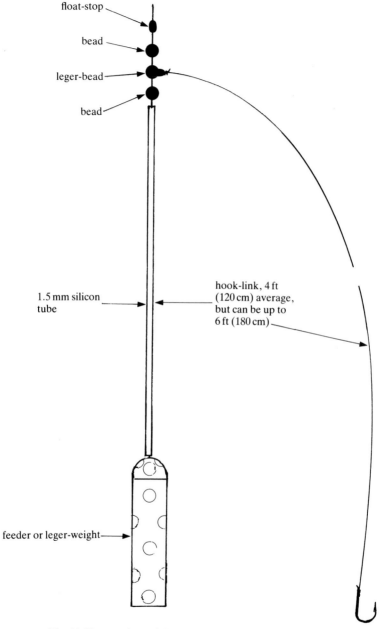

Fig. 11. Non-tangle revolving paternoster for feeder and leger.

to 5 or 6 feet—but only rarely have I found that to be necessary. Conversely, if fish are deep-hooked, shorten the hook-link a little. Get the 'fine-tuning' right and you will get easy-to-hit bites—guaranteed!

I have heard it said that my approach does not solve the problem at all; some twitcher-fans have suggested that my long hook-links merely camouflage the problem in that twitch-bites do not show and the only bites I see are those than come from the occasional suicidal fish that feed without caution.

This argument falls down due to the simple fact that the 'twitcher-hitters' do not get more bites than I do. I get as many (or as few—depending on the enthusiasm of the tench!) as they do. But I catch far more tench than they do because virtually every one of the bites I receive results in a tench on the bank.

Actually it is a bit pretentious of me to refer to 'my approach' because it is not really anything of the sort. It is actually a modification of Ivan Marks' approach—when I read his comments on legering for bream in the Relief Channel (this was in the days when it contained bream—before the zander ate them all—sic!) in his book on match fishing, it made good, sound sense to me ... as indeed it might, after all the man won the Relief Channel Championship 3 years out of 4! So I applied his approach to my own bream fishing and, encouraged by its success, applied it to my tench fishing too.

It worked. Thanks Ivan!

So Ivan's basic approach was married with an east coast beach-fishing rig (revolving swivel rig), and I came up with my version of the fixed-paternoster.

An incidental lesson to be learned from the development of 'my approach', is that we can often profit from the experience of those involved in spheres of angling other than our own. My reading of match fishing literature combined with my experience of beach fishing for cod, enabled me to develop a highly effective rig and approach for tench.

The feeders I prefer are Drennan Feederlinks—but I use them upside-down and capless so they become semi open-ended.

The lead, usually one of the smaller Feederlink weights, is enclosed inside the feeder and retained in position with a split-ring (Fig. 12).

I prefer semi open-ended feeders to block-ends, incidentally, because the bait releases more readily and the groundbait used to plug the feeder has its own inherent appeal.

Generally I will fish with 2 feeder rods—they may be cast different distances, to different depths or to different features.

With lightly weighted feeders I like to use ultra-light ring-type bobbin indicators—to prevent them swinging in a wind I hang them over double-ended knitting-needles stuck in the ground.

I invariably use electronic bite-alarms in conjection with bobbin

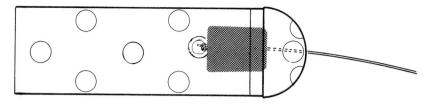

Fig. 12. Capless Drennan 'Feederlink' used semi open-ended and weighted inside.

indicators, this releases my attention and enables me to relax a bit and watch the water, or read ... or sun-bathe, instead of staring fixedly at a couple of indicators which, let us be honest, until they start moving, are not the most fascinating objects in the world!

A cross-wind will belly the line and pull a lightly-weighted feeder out of position so it is necessary to sink the line as quickly (but gently) as possible. After casting I therefore put the rod in the rests and hang a washing-up liquid bottle-top, into which a small lead has been pressed, between butt and second ring. Every time the bobbin falls to the ground I wind it back up to the rod—when it stops falling I know the slack has gone so I remove the weighted-bobbin and replace it with the ring-indicator.

If the wind is really troublesome and you are aware that the feeder is being shifted out of position, you can either load the feeder with a slightly heavier weight or put a couple of drops of washing-up liquid on the coils of line on the spool just before casting. I carry a little eye-dropper bottle of washing-up liquid in it for this purpose. A 'soaped' line will sink much more readily than an untreated one.

I always fish feeders with the pick-ups closed and the anti-reverse disengaged (ie with the reels in 'spin'). When a bite occurs I grasp the rod handle, drop a finger to the reel-flier to prevent an overrun, and gently strike. Sometimes the takes are slow, leisurely affairs that give you all the time in the world, but at least as frequent are those that cause the indicator to fly up to the rod and set the reel spinning. Both are equally easy to deal with—just take your time and do not be panicked into making too hard a strike.

Exactly the same terminal tackle is used for light-legering—the only difference being that the feeder is replaced with the appropriate size weight—usually half to three-quarters of an ounce.

The decision whether to use a feeder or leger depends mainly on casting range—the leger is much more aerodynamic than the feeder so casts further. It also depends on how frequently I expect to get bites—if I expect to have to wait a long time for a bite I do not really see the point of using a feeder because it works best when it is recast fairly frequently. Normally, though, I opt for the feeder because range is only rarely a major factor, and the fully loaded feeder provides an 'amplified signal' to which the tench can home-in. This, I believe, increases the chances of the hook-bait being located.

To translate theory into practice I would like to describe an actual session—it was an early morning, pre-work session and occurred one July weekday morning. It was a few years ago because in recent seasons most of my waters have become so heavily weeded that light-line fishing is impractical.

Details
Rods: Two. 11 ft, 1¼ lb test-curve
Reels: Mitchell 410A
Line: Sylcast, 5 lb test
Hook: Size 12, Sealey 1714B (no longer available)
Hook-link: Sylcast, 4 lb test
Terminal tackle: Fixed paternoster (knot version), Drennan Feeder
Bait: Redworm
Groundbait: Cereal (as per recipe in bait chapter) and maggots

4.00 am The weather is cool and overcast with a moderate south-west wind. I choose a swim that is 12 feet deep straight out and shelves up to about 6 feet in a two o'clock direction. Before tackling-up I fire 3 tangerine-size balls of maggot-laced groundbait straight out, to 12 ft of water, and 3 balls to midway between one and two o'clock where the depth is about 8 feet. I try to put each 3-ball batch in a triangular configuration—not too difficult to achieve because the range is only about 30 metres.

My tackle is set up and the first rod baited with a redworm. The worm is hooked head-end only, I have found this far superior to any other method. The feeder is crammed with maggots and plugged with groundbait. I jam the plug in hard, otherwise the maggots will start to crawl out before I cast.

The rod is propped up on a rest, ensuring that the loaded feeder does not dangle in the water, and I fire out another maggot-laced groundbait ball to the baited area. The feeder rod is picked up and cast to the centre of the spreading rings. The rationale behind this is that with a given pull of the catapult, a groundbait ball will always go more or less the same distance—and the spreading rings identify the range for me. With practice is works well and ensures that feed and end-tackle always go to the same area.

A weighted bottle-top is hung between butt and second ring to sink the line while I attend to the second rod.

A 7 lb 5 oz tench is landed—it took a worm-baited feeder. In those days I used
a keepnet—I no longer use one—ever.

Whack!

The weighted bobbin has shot up to the rod and the reel is spinning
like a food-whisk! I grab the rod, drop a finger on the reel-flier to stop
it spinning and strike. The rod hoops over and a fish is on. It does not
feel like a tench though . . . everything falls slack—it has gone.

Pike! I bet it was a pike. I retrieve. The hook has gone and the
end of the hook-link has some distinct 'fret-saw' notches in it. Undoubtedly a pike.

A new hook is tied on. I rebait, reload the feeder, catapult a new
groundbait ball and recast. The right-hand rod likewise. Both lines are
sunk and ring-indicators hung in position.

6.20 am Twitchy take on left-hand rod. I strike—the rod hoops over
as before but this time it stays on—and *does* feel like a tench. No it
doesn't. It swings round fast to the left—I think it is a small carp.

It isn't. It is a pike! About 9 lb I would guess—probably the one
that gave me a bite-off earlier—no sign of the previous hook though.

The pike is returned—I check the hook-link, it seems to be un-damaged.

Rebait, reload the feeder, fire out another groundbait ball and recast.

The right hand rod is away! It is a reel-spinner. Drop a finger on the flier and rod up ... oh yes, this is more like it! It moves slowly to the right, lodges briefly in some sparse weed strands but soon comes free. Playing big tench on this light tackle is lovely—I can feel every lunge and have to respond to every pull. Slowly, gradually, the fish comes to the margins—there is a bit more weed here, I must be careful.

Gently does it ... over the net ... I sigh with relief—only now realising that I am gritting my teeth and holding my breath.

7 lb 6 oz. It goes in the keepsack.

A new groundbait ball and a recast follow. Time for a coffee, then I shall set up the camera for a picture. A tench rolls over the left-hand baited area, the pike hot-spot(!)—that is the second time this morning. I bet I get a take on that rod.

7.10 am   What a take! I did not see it go—one moment everything was quiet and still, next instant the indicator was tight to the rod and the alarm was screeching! The strike was instinctive—I cannot remember doing it, but here I am with a bent rod in my hands. This is another big one—oh yes, it's making me backwind. Now it is swinging to the left—don't go too far please, there is a big weed bed there, and a trailing willow with lots of roots in the water.

That's better—it's my side of the weeds and seems to be tiring. I play it gently—if I do not give it too much to fight against it may stay calm ... it's over the net and ... it's in!

7 lb 2 oz. Another sack is wetted, in the margins it goes. Two anglers arrive behind me—they agree to take a few pictures for me.

7.30 am   It is now time to pack up or I shall be late for work. The kids will have a tired but good-humoured teacher today!

Hang on! A take to the rod that is still fishing ... I strike ... it's on—but it is not a tench. It feels quite heavy, but there is no fight to it—it feels breamy.

And so it proves—6 lb-ish I would guess—and back it goes.

A 9 lb pike, two 7 lb plus tench and a 6 lb bream—all before work. If only I did not have to go to work ... I bet there would be more fish today ... I canvas my system for an ailment that will enable me to 'phone in sick with a clear conscience. No suitable ailment is found! Perhaps if I concentrate really hard on my sinuses I might detect the beginnings of a sinus-induced headache—the embryonic beginnings of something that will become ever more debilitating as the day progresses ...

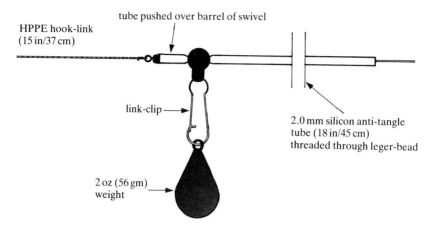

tube pushed over barrel of swivel

HPPE hook-link
(15 in/37 cm)

link-clip

2.0 mm silicon anti-tangle
tube (18 in/45 cm)
threaded through leger-bead

2 oz (56 gm)
weight

Fig. 13. Anti-tangle fixed-lead rig.

I resist the temptation and load my gear in the car.
I'll go to heaven for sure!

Standard Legering

Where weed conditions are such that light hook-links are impractical, I do not use a feeder because I do not think it is possible to achieve good presentation with small, light baits like redworms unless a fine line and lightweight hook are used. In weedy swims, therefore, I use what are, in effect, scaled-down carp tactics. But do not interpret that phrase 'scaled-down' too literally because although tench do not grow anywhere near as large as carp, they are far more difficult to deal with in weed. The tackle *must* be strong enough to free a weeded fish so I regard 8 lb test as the absolute minimum, and generally use 9 lb. I realise that some tench anglers will flinch at the prospect of using what they see as excessively heavy tackle—but the use of anything lighter is irresponsible. In this sort of circumstance we have to base line strength not so much on the size of the fish we are hoping to catch, but on the conditions that exist in the swim.

In conjunction with my 8 or 9 lb line I use 1¾ lb test-curve rods and a fixed-lead terminal tackle.

The fixed-lead rig is identical to the one I use for my carp fishing and in various forms has been described by a number of writers, but for the benefit of those who may not be familiar with it, I have illustrated it in Fig. 13. The accompanying caption details the rig's component parts.

The only element that requires additional description is the line-

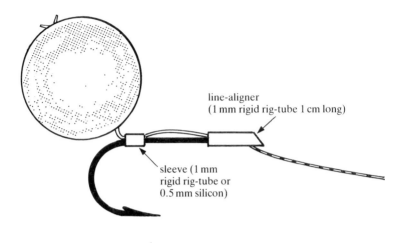

line-aligner
(1 mm rigid rig-tube 1 cm long)

sleeve (1 mm
rigid rig-tube or
0.5 mm silicon)

Detail of line-aligner showing
how aligner is jammed over
hook-eye, and hook-link
emerges from tiny hole

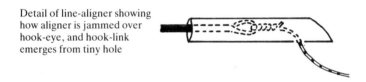

Fig. 14. Line-aligner to increase likelihood of self-hooking.

aligner (Fig. 14). The rationale behind the aligner is a development that owes its origins to modern carp angling. The drawing makes the arrangement clearer than could words. The 1 mm rigid rig-tube is about 1 cm long, and the hook-link is threaded through with a darning-needle before the swivel is tied on. When the aligner is jammed over the hook-eye (it must be a ring or straight-eyed hook), the hook-link emerges from the front of the aligner which, coupled with the use of an ultra-soft hook-link such as Silkworm or Gamabraid, ensures that the hook will turn and snag as it is drawn over the fish's lip.

The principle is the same as that claimed for the bent-hook rig, but frankly I doubt that the bent-hook rig works in the way its fans imagine ... but that is another matter and beyond the scope of this particular discussion. The principle being that no matter which way the hook is facing, it will always turn and snag when the hook-link is drawn taut to the fixed-lead.

Seven something. It was returned very hastily because another run occurred while the picture was being taken!

This day produced one of just over 8 lb and another of seven plus. I'm not sure which one this is.

A 7 lb 4 oz winter fish that was caught on worm and feeder.

A factor six day! I am not sure who is the slipperiest, me or the tench! It weighed 6-10.

I remember that this was a pre-work fish but cannot for the life of me recall what it weighed.

A lovely looking seven-plus goes back.

Above Nearly a two-tone tench, one of very few I have caught that displayed this sort of colour-range.

Below A brace of big ones caught on feeder tackle. The one I'm holding weighed 7 lb 15 oz. An ounce more and it would have been my first eight pounder ... How close can you get!

An absolutely gorgeous primrose coloured tench – some of these gravel-pit fish are unbelievably beautiful.

An early morning seven-plus, unusually it came before the sun was up.

My 8 lb 6 oz fish and the mini-boilies that were used as loose-feed; particles were used on the hook.

Tench weather! And judging from the drying sacks and weigh-bag it was a successful one (I don't remember).

Try this simple test. Rig any straight-eyed hook with a line-aligner, then drape it over your finger. Now try to pull the hook over your finger ...you will find that it will turn and snag, no matter which way it happens to be facing.

Does it make much difference? Frankly, no! I miss very few tench takes without the aligner, so the aligner was certainly not born out of necessity ... but my carp fishing experience convinces me that it is such an efficient system that it cannot possibly have a detrimental effect when used for tench fishing. So I'll not give you any 'hype' and claim that this is some sort of wonder-rig that will revolutionise your fishing, because it will not—but it just might put the occasional extra fish on the bank that might otherwise be missed. That is all I claim.

The bulk of my standard legering is with boilies or particles—and taken overall I would recommend smallish (14 mm) boilies as being the most effective.

As I did with feeder-fishing, I shall put 'flesh on the bones' by describing an actual session. It occurred one hot, sunny day last August ('89). The water was a gravel-pit of about 15 acres.

Details
Rods: Two. 11 ft, 1¾ lb test-curve
Reels: Mitchell 410A
Line: Sylcast, 9 lb test
Hook: Mustad 34021, size 6
Hook-link: 15 lb Silkworm, 15 inches long
Terminal tackle: Fixed-lead (2 ounce lead)
Bait: 14 mm fish-meal boilies (see bait chapter for recipe)
Groundbait: Hook-bait boilies

5.30 am The weather forecast has promised a light southerly breeze so I make my way round to the north bank—the breeze will then be directly in my face. An angler is in the swim, he has been there all night, but he is in the process of packing up. I decide to wait. We chat while he packs away his gear and it transpires that he has had a blank night.

To the left of this swim is a wasps' nest—last time out I was stung on the hand, so I have come prepared and take from my ruck-sack a small bottle of carbon tetrachloride and a piece of rag. The rag is soaked in the liquid and with the aid of a stick, poked down the wasp-hole. A big clod of earth is then placed over the hole to keep the fumes and the wasps inside. The bottle is then wrapped in a poly-bag and checked to ensure that it is properly sealed. Carbon tetrachloride fumes are *very* dangerous and if inhaled can kill.

A few wasps that had already left the nest before I dealt with it start hovering round the sealed entrance—they will get the 'hump' as the day progresses and may be a bit of a nuisance. They will not be

23 inches long and a weight of seven-plus. Imagine what it would have weighed with a bellyful of spawn!

a problem after today though.

Having dealt with the wasps, I set up my gear. My rods are pre-rigged so it only takes a few moments to have them ready. Bank-sticks, buzzer-bars, alarms and monkey-climbers are set up too. As is the landing net.

About 30 metres out, slightly to my right, is an island. There are a few weed-free patches on the slope of the island and it is to one of these that I intend casting my right-hand rod. I know where the clear patches are because it is a swim I know well and one in which I have kept track of weed encroachment.

The 2½ cm hair is baited with 2 boilies—a pop-up and normal sinker on the same hair. As well as creating a nearly neutral-density bait, it sits up nicely on the bottom and seems to be a presentation that tench find particularly appealing. To the hook is attached a 4-bait stringer. Why 4? Well, 6 is my lucky number ... and 2 baits on the hair, plus 4 on the stringer makes 6 ... Philistines among you may dismiss that as illogical, superstitious nonsense. I would agree with you! But *I* believe

METHODS AND TACTICS 83

in it, and that is what matters!

The tackle is cast to the appropriate spot but, as always when fishing small holes in weed, there is a momentary crisis of confidence as I ask myself the question, 'Was that a tiny bit too close to the island? Shall I retrieve and recast? ... No, dammit no. Leave it where it is. Pander to that "Shall I recast?" nonsense and I'll be forever winding it back and chucking it back out.' (Angling authors have crises of confidence you see!)

Some anglers like to give the tackle a pull and see if it is on clear ground—I figure that such an action is as likely to pull the bait *into* weed as reveal whether or not it is in the clear, so I leave it where it lands.

You have to discipline yourself when fishing clear spots in the weed—if you fail to impose self-discipline you get paranoid and spend more time casting than fishing.

My left-hand rod is baited up in identical fashion. I want to cast this one just beyond and slightly to one side of an underwater hump. I cannot see the hump but from previous sessions I know towards which far-bank marker I need to aim. Range is more difficult—it is done by 'feel'—in this instance it is a sort of 'medium overhand lob'. Again there is the niggle about whether or not the tackle has landed in weed or the clear—but again I refuse to pander to the doubt that wants to gnaw at my confidence.

Twenty or so freebie-boilies are catapulted to the vicinity of each bait. The gulls home-in on the sound of the catapult almost immediately but by using a pouch-type catapult and firing out 5 baits at a time, the gulls rarely get more than one or maybe 2 from each batch.

Before sitting back and relaxing, I check that everything is in order: alarms are switched on, medium-weight monkeys are set halfway up the needles so they will record drop-backs as well as runs, pick-ups are opened and the lines placed in clips just forward of the reels.

By now (7.00 am-ish) the sun has a fair bit of warmth—later it will almost certainly be a shorts and sun-cream day. I sit on the bed-chair, pour a cup of coffee and 'have an enjoy'. It is lovely to be here—only one other angler on the lake, and he is way down the far end. If I could be anyone in the whole world, I'd be myself, here, now. Do people other than anglers ever experience such a fulfilling sense of well-being I wonder?

The tench are late-starters here; I could get a take at about 9.00 am, but on recent form I think 11.00 am-ish is much more likely.

10.30 am A run to the right-hand rod! The alarm is screeching its shrill note and the monkey is flying up and down the needle. Close bale, wind down tight and strike! It is in weed. It always happens in this swim—I cannot recall a single fish that was not in weed when hooked. This is always the worrying time—there is a criss-cross cat's-cradle of line in the weed because too many anglers fish too light for the conditions and break-off. If I get snagged in that stuff, I'll lose the fish. No, not this time. It comes free, sheds the weed and starts fighting.

7 lb 5 oz—and not a trace of spawn. A beautiful fish. A couple of self-taken pictures with the Minolta's self-timer and it is returned to the water.

1.30 pm Another run—again it is the right-hand rod. Again I have to heave it free of the weed before I can enjoy the fight. This one is a bit smaller at 6 lb 10 oz, but it qualifies for a picture because of its beautiful primrose colouring. These gravel-pit tench are amazing animals—the colours sometimes beyond belief.

1.45 pm Whilst rebaiting the right-hand rod, the left-hand one is away. I hook the fish but it is solid in the weed and cat's-cradled mono, and all attempts to free it fail. Eventually the hook pulls free.

I wish anglers would choose tackle for the *conditions* rather than just the size of the fish.

I fish on until about teatime but receive no more action. A couple of tench roll close-in and I contemplate dropping a bait in the spot, but my coffee-flask is empty, my sandwiches have been eaten and I am starting to think longing thoughts about a plate of pasta and a Valpolicella.

It has been a good day. The spaghetti and wine will round it off perfectly—so I pack up. As always I leave the baits in the water until the very last moment, but there is no last-minute run today.

I wonder how big was the one I lost?

Heavy Legering

A feature of recent years is that many of our waters have been getting progressively weedier—some are so densely weeded that we are forced to completely revise our thoughts on what constitutes suitable tackle for tench. In a few waters, where the tench run very large and the weed is particularly bad, I use 12 lb line—and even with tackle *that* heavy I have had a few touch-and-go moments when it has been a close-run thing between a weeded tench coming free or my line breaking.

Contrary to what you might imagine, this does not result in damage to the mouth of a hooked fish—this is because most of the force being applied is taken by the weed and not by the fish itself. As evidence of this I would cite how difficult it can be to heave terminal tackle out of the weed when it snarls up during the course of an ordinary fishless retrieve. With my hand on my heart I can say that not once, when employ-

Big, black and ugly—a big male tench.

ing these seemingly heavy-handed tactics, have I caused damage to a tench's mouth. Were it ever to happen, I would no longer fish this way. But that, in truth, would mean that some swims in some waters would then become unfishable because to use lighter tackle would result in a high proportion of fish hooked being lost.

So I shall complete this trilogy of actual trips by describing an example of heavy fishing in a deep and extremely weedy 12-acre pit that holds some very large, but rarely caught tench.

As in the previous two examples it is a record of events exactly as they occurred. Obviously it is an account of a successful session, but do not run away with the idea that I am always whipping the water to a froth while pulling out tench—sometimes I know the weather is wrong and I know a blank is on the cards; often I am unable to get the swim I want, nor even my second or third choice so I am compelled to fish where I know my chances of success are slim. Sometimes the weather is perfect and I am in the swim I want, but fishing is sabotaged by the arrival of an angler (?) next door who proceeds to embark on 45 minutes solid hammering with a steel-headed mallet in setting up his pitch.

Don't you just love 'em to death!

But despite all these frustrations there are occasions, and in truth they are frequent enough, when everything comes right—and on such days the indicators usually fly.

This is an account of one such day—and as with the previous account, it occurred in August of that wonderful summer of '89.

Details
Rods: Three. 11 ft, 2¼ lb test-curve
Reels: Mitchell 410A
Line: Maxima, 12 lb test on one rod; Sylcast 11 lb test on the other two
Hook: Mustad 34021, size 6
Hook-link: 15 lb Silkworm, 15 inches long
Terminal tackle: Fixed-lead (2 ounce lead)
Bait: 14 mm fish-meal boilies on two rods, 14 mm bun-spice boilie on third
Groundbait: 50/50 mix of hemp and tares plus a small quantity of maple peas; also some hook-bait samples

4.30 am   The forecasters have promised a hot, sunny day—as has been the pattern this remarkable summer. I make my way to the 'In-Willows' swim—on this water and in these weather conditions it is my favourite tench swim; it is, however, a difficult swim to fish effectively because there are very few clear-spots as such, rather there are spots where the weed is thin enough to permit satisfactory bait-presentation.

One bait is cast just 5 or 6 feet from the margins; the middle rod is cast about 4 feet beyond it, and the third is cast to the bottom of the marginal slope. Before casting, each hook-point is PVA'd to prevent a hang-up occurring in weed for, as already stated, none of the spots are completely weed-free. Fishing depths are about 6 ft, 10 ft and 15 ft.

About 4 ounces of the hemp/tares mixture is thrown or catapulted round each bait. A couple of ounces of maple peas are thrown round each hook-bait too, along with half a dozen hook-bait samples.

All 3 rods are fished with slack lines; I do not worry about anti-tangle tubes rising vertically from the leads because I am convinced that they are unlikely to cause alarm in the jungle of weeds that covers the bed of the swim. Did I say, 'Covers the bed'?—that is rather misleading because despite the depth of water (it averages approximately 17 ft) many of the weed-strands rise all the way to the surface.

To ensure slack lines, the monkeys are allowed to rest at the bottom of the needles.

6.30 am   A tench rolls just beyond the position fished by the third (deepest) rod. A carp jumps about 30 metres out.

7.00 am Masses of bubbles appear just beyond the marginal weed. I speculate about the likelihood of them being due to foraging tench. Frankly, I have my doubts—I have seen identical bubbling in swims where I could actually see the bottom and fish have not been responsible.

8.10 am The close-in (right-hand) rod stabs down, the buzzer screams and the monkey does its thing. I close the bale, strike and I'm in! There are a few heavy lunges then everything goes solid. Past experience has taught me that there is no point waiting for the fish to free itself—so I gradually increase the pressure, thankful that I am using gear capable of withstanding the loading I am giving it. Then slowly, ever so slowly, I feel some movement. I gain a yard or so of line but can feel no animated movement on the end. Yes I can! There is a lunge, then another—now it swings to the left and clumps of elodea appear on the surface. The fish is now virtually free of weed and is pulling hard—some of the lunges are vicious and the clutch gives a brief snarl in response. It would be lovely to let this fish have its head and run, but if I give it the chance it will dive straight into the weed again.

It is on a short line now, but I still have not seen it. Then I glimpse it—it looks good, not enormous, but good. It rolls—oh yes, a lovely fish, definitely a seven plus.

I try to steer it to the net and, at the same time, keep it clear of the other two lines—the fish is having none of it and goes berserk, picking up the middle line in the process and adding a sense of urgency to the situation by making the buzzer sound.

I draw it over the net and ... got it! I unhook it in the margins, the hook being so firmly embedded that I have to use forceps ... there was no way that fish would have come adrift! It is placed in a pre-wetted keepsack while I sort out the auto-everything compact camera—set on self-timer mode it will focus, select the appropriate exposure and even switch on the flash if conditions require it. One friend reckons I could equip it with a little pair of wellies and it would even go out and catch the fish for me and eliminate the need for me to spend all those fruitless hours beside windswept gravel-pits!

After taking a couple of photographs I weigh the fish, 7 lb 10 oz, and notice for the umpteenth time how even fish of this size seem to 'shrink' when viewed from above. It dives down into the weed, leaving me to sort out the two tangled rods. Had the swim been weed-free I could have avoided tangles by using slide-down leads (described in 'Big-Water Carp'), but in weed they cannot work efficiently and can actually compound the problem by snagging.

It is nearly 9 o'clock before I manage to get both rods sorted out and recast. A few more handfuls of hemp and tares are scattered round the near bait.

Carp-style fishing; but big tench are the quarry.

11.00 am   Same rod, another run. Events much as before except that I manage to avoid tangles. It weighs just over 7¼ lb.

12.15 pm   A flier on the middle rod—it results in a lapful of hook-link material, hooks and dental-floss (I was tying-up hook-links) being dumped on the bed-chair. I close the bale, wind down and strike ... Hell! That is a savage lunge! Briefly I wonder if it is a carp—but such thoughts are soon dispelled because the fight is characteristic of a big tench, including the unceremonious haul from the weeds!

It weighs 8 lb 2 oz, my third 8-plus of the season. What a summer—the carp will have to wait longer than usual this year!

2.00 pm   No more takes have occurred—I pour the last of my coffee and watch the coots diving over my groundbait—they were attracted by the floating weed, found the groundbait and are now being an absolute pain ... I conclude that it is time to pack up. It has been a fabulous day—only once have I taken more 7-plusses in a day, that was two seasons earlier when I had 4 over 7 (including an 8) in a morning. As I emerge from the shade of the willows I am made aware of how hot the day has become. Tench love a heatwave, especially if, as today, there is a breeze ruffling the surface.

As I open the car door I step back to avoid the oven-blast of hot air that gushes out. I slowly pack my tackle as a Cortina pulls up alongside—the first of the weekend carp-boys has arrived. 'Any good?' he asks.

'No,' I reply.

'Too hot I reckon,' he says.

"Probably."

It does not pay to draw undue attention to success—at least, not until it is over!

Postscript

Hawk-eyed readers will have noticed a paradox—a contradiction in my advice regarding the methods I employ for catching big tench.

In the section on feeder-fishing I laid great emphasis on the fact that the way to avoid twitch-bites was to use a long hook-link; whilst in the medium and heavy legering sections I recommended a hook-link of about 15 inches.

Why the difference?

The difference is in the baits used. For feeder fishing I use small baits—my choice, as already stated, being small worms. Small baits seem to encourage delicate feeding—so much so that too heavy a hook-link or too heavy a hook and the bait will be rejected—if indeed it gets taken at all. The sort of baits used on my medium and heavy outfits, by contrast, are relatively large—boilies and particles for example. My usual choice being two 14 mm boilies, one pop-up and one sinker, used together. Such a bait represents a substantial mouthful, and the sort of feeding that such baits induce is far less delicate and subtle than that encountered with mini-baits. The shorter hook-link, therefore, works satisfactorily. I have tried longer hook-links with boilies but have not found that they offer any advantage at all. There is, however, a lower limit, and I do not recommend hook-links shorter than about 12 inches, even with boilies. Short hook-links of less than 6 inches can work well for carp, but I do not recommend them for tench—the way they take a bait is different to the way carp take a bait and ultra-short hook-links are not, therefore, appropriate. My choice, based on a lot of experiment, is for something between 12 and 18 inches—with 15 inches striking me as optimum.

But as I said earlier, in a different context, 'Don't take my word for it'—conduct your own experiments and form your own conclusions. What I say is not important, nor is what others say important—the arbiters of the correctness of an approach are the tench. If your indicators fly with regularity and you are putting tench on the bank, you are doing it right. The methods I have described result in my indicators flying with satisfying regularity—I am confident that 'my' methods will work for you too—but they *may* need modification on your waters, and I would be the last to claim that 'my' methods cannot be improved upon … mind you, I think you will have to go some!

Big Tench

Just how big is big?

I am prompted to ask the question because every summer we see a crop of grotesquely bloated tench in the press; fish that weigh much more than they ought to weigh due to their carrying an enormous amount of spawn. Quite modest fish can become 'big' if we use weight as the sole criterion—while tench that are already big become positively enormous. A case in point being the current record (14 lb 3 oz, Mr P. Gooriah, Wraysbury Pit, 1987).

I mean no disrespect to the captor of that tench when I say that all the photographs I have seen of the fish make it obvious that its weight was unnaturally enhanced by its carrying an exceptional and excessive weight of spawn. Frankly, I think the poor thing was an obscene parody of a tench and with my hand on my heart I can truthfully say that I would not wish to catch it, nor any similarly distorted specimen.

If we fish for tench in June and July there is no way we are going to be able to avoid catching tench with well-rounded, spawn-filled bellies—but the likelihood of catching the distended specimens that are bloated out of all proportion to their length is, thankfully, slight. Strangely it seems to be a phenomenon that is largely confined to a few waters where excessive bloating seems to be a characteristic of early-season fish.

No 'normal' tench will ever topple the current record—the only fish likely to do so is another overblown football shaped specimen. And this, I feel, is unfortunate—it strikes me as being on par with an athlete breaking the javelin record by throwing while there is a gale blowing from behind, or a boxer winning a fight with weights in his gloves. Whilst I do not doubt for one moment that the current record tench was caught by fair angling, I feel that we have to have criteria other than that of weight alone.

Look, for example, at the ludicrous situation with regard to rainbow trout. The record is meaningless, it being a record of animal husbandry and nothing whatsoever to do with angling.

And what about a pike that on initial weighing beats the record, but before being weighed again in front of witnesses regurgitates some

Unhooking a big tench.

partially digested fish? Which weight should qualify? Especially if the second weight puts it below the record? Supposing a pike was caught that had the tail of a 5 lb jack protruding from its throat. Should it count as caught, or should the jack be removed?

There are those who maintain that a record list is merely a record of history—but it should be meaningful history if it is to mean anything at all—otherwise it is not worth recording.

In my opinion, therefore, a record fish should not have its weight disproportionately enhanced by spawn or stomach contents. Nor should an artificially-reared specimen qualify.

I realise that my contention causes problems—like when is spawn-weight 'normal'? When do stomach contents qualify as disproportionate? And how long after its release can a stew-pond fish be reasonably regarded as natural?

Of course there will be difficult, borderline decisions—but as regards the current record tench, I have no doubts at all that it was grotesquely deformed and should not qualify as a record.

So, to return to the question with which I started this chapter—'How big is big?'

My opinion, bearing in mind that I live near some of the best tench waters in the country, is that a 6 lb tench is big and a 7-pounder is huge. Some of you, on reading that last statement will be asking, 'What is this man on?'—believing that my perspectives must have been distorted by some substance that affects my perception of reality! I concede that it must be difficult to accept that a tench has to reach 6 lb to be classed as big when you have never seen anything much over 4 lb in the whole of your angling career. But taken nationally, it is a simple fact that one-time specimens of 4 and 5 lb can no longer be considered as anything other than very run-of-the-mill.

So what has happened? Why are modern-day tench so much larger than they used to be?

A number of theories have been put forward to explain the phenomenon—ranging from the pretentious presumption that it has been due to the development of modern angling methods, to the naive belief that it is due to boilies providing a sudden influx of high-quality supplementary food.

Neither theory withstands even the most casual scrutiny so I shall not afford them the dignity of argument. What we are seeing is, in fact, a phenomenon that has come about due to a combination of circumstances. Briefly, and somewhat over-simplified I admit, the sequence of events has been thus:

1. Many new gravel-pits were created in the post-war years; a practice

This gravel-pit, photographed while it was being dug, is now flooded and holds some big tench.

that has continued (with occasional hiccups as the demand for aggregates varied) to the present day.

2. New gravel-pits were (and are) relatively inhospitable environments—those of us who fished them prior to the mid-70's know that many of them were relatively weed-free and as a consequence were relatively barren of food.

3. Due to their inhospitable nature and limited food supplies, fish stocks tended to be relatively low. Lack of weed (and consequent lack of spawning/nursery areas) contributed to fish stocks remaining low.

4. Low numbers meant that despite limited overall food supplies, per-capita food supplies were adequate for reasonable and sometimes good growth.

5. Changing agricultural practices, notably the increasing use of agro-chemicals to satisfy the demands of intensive arable farming, led to water-soluble nitrates contaminating the water-table and finding their way into our gravel-pits.

6. The contamination of the water-table with nitrates, something that greatly worries ecologists (sufficiently for there to be an EEC proposal to limit its use) has led to a dramatic enrichment of our pits and an unprecedented increase in per-capita food availability.

Rapid growth was and is the result.

But nature does not leave ecological niches unfilled for long and signs are that those once sparsely-stocked waters are now becoming tenanted by increased fish populations—which in the long-term will result in per-capita food supplies reverting to something a bit closer to normal.

So, if you want to catch some big tench, my advice is that you do it *now*. The bubble *will* burst and I predict that within a tench-generation or two we will be looking back on the 80's and 90's as the boom years for big tench.

One of the most important lessons I have learned in angling is that good times do not last forever. We have the good fortune to be living in a time when big tench are more plentiful than they have ever been, and more plentiful than they will be at any time in the future.

Someone will quote those words in years to come and will say, 'He was right, you know.'

But before we get carried away with our enthusiasm, let me establish a few perspectives. As I said earlier, a 6 lb tench is big and a 7-pounder is huge. To continue the progression I will say that 8-pounders are positively enormous and are very rare.

So where do all those 8-pounders in the press come from?

I shall whisper a little secret to you—an awful lot of them do not weigh 8 lb!

The simple truth of the matter is that a lot of tench are, shall we say, weighed somewhat optimistically.

Some are weighed *very* optimistically!

Does it matter?

Not really—except that the true position becomes hopelessly distorted and gives anglers unrealistic expectations. I doubt if more than 10% of reported 8-pounders actually weigh over 8 lb. Yes, I would put the figure as low as that. In general I put far more store by the stated weights of big tench captured accidentally by carp anglers, than the weights claimed by tench anglers. This apparent paradox is due to few carp anglers being desperate to catch an 8 lb tench, whereas most tench anglers regard such a fish as their ultimate ambition—the absolute zenith, as it were. This enthusiasm leads them to, as I put it earlier, weigh 'optimistically'.

Or exaggerate.

Or lie!

Have I made my point?

So, where do we look for 6 and 7 lb tench (having accepted that 8-pounders are very rare animals indeed)?

Although they can and do occasionally come from natural lakes and canals, I would advise the would-be big-tench angler to look to gravel-pits. Some reservoirs, due to the aforementioned nitrate situation, have the potential too, but as a rule-of-thumb I would advise looking to gravel-pits. In particular I would look to relatively large gravel-pits (say, over 10 acres), and even more particularly to those that are deep, clear and heavily weeded.

Yes, I know that big tench can come from small, shallow, murky and virtually weed-free pits, I can think of one such as I write, but if I advised you to look to such waters I would seriously mislead you. So—big, deep, clear and weedy are the characteristics you should look for.

It would be inappropriate of me to name big-tench waters—besides, some of the best known are mentioned quite readily in the angling press and as a result are already overcrowded. What I shall do instead is give you a few 'pointers' that will enable you to find quiet, and even unexploited and hitherto unknown waters.

I recommend that you look especially closely at gravel-pits in the valleys of the Thames and its tributaries. Many of them are club owned, some may have geographical limits on membership or have long waiting-lists, but very many of them can be joined without difficulty. Alternatively you can join one of the commercial schemes like Leisure Sport—anyone who buys a Leisure Sport general permit will have access to some of the best tench waters in the country. No, I will not tell you which ones are particularly good for the simple and selfish reason that I fish some of them myself—but rest assured you would have access to enough waters of known (and as yet unknown) potential to see you into the next century. And that is not a commercial 'plug', I have no financial interest in the Leisure Sport organisation, but I do appreciate the excellent fishing they make available.

Doubtless other commercial fishery organisations have good waters too, but I have no direct experience on which to draw so cannot make further recommendations. But that is the lovely thing about tench fishing—there are many waters of superb big-tench potential yet to be discovered. Everyone these days wants to be a carp angler, so tench are neglected—this means that some of the top waters in the country are accessible to anyone for the price of a ticket.

One of my favourite techniques for finding big-tench waters is to capitalise on what I call the 'sponge syndrome'. There are some waters that attract a lot of angling pressure—nearby there can be other waters that are virutally ignored. Sometimes, not always by any means, the neglected water has as much or nearly as much potential as the hard-fished water. Waters situated fairly close together often share similar physical and chemical characteristics with the result that they can often share the same potential for producing big fish—but anglers on the whole are not particularly imaginative and tend to return time and again to the known waters, the ones with the proven track-record.

Having identified a potential big-tench water I would want to visit it in the latter part of the close-season. Ideally I would choose a hot, sunny day. If there is a reasonable population of tench in the water, I would expect to see them. As well as classic rolling and tail-flapping, I would expect to see small groups of pre-spawners swimming along the margins. Unlike carp that tend to mass-up, tench are more likely to be seen in twos and threes; there will be loners too. They will not be gently meandering but will be swimming quickly and purposefully, but despite this apparent determination to get wherever they are going, you will find that they are merely patrolling up and down the same length of bank. They will do this for hours on end—sometimes for days on end.

Not all tench in a water will behave this way at any one time because, again unlike carp that demonstrate spawning behaviour en-masse, tench seem to spawn a few at a time. Nor do they necessarily get it done in one frenzied session—but will seemingly shed some spawn, go quiet for a while, then shed some more ... and so on. I get the impression that it is by no means unusual for individual females to shed their spawn in several small batches.

What this means is that although you should be able to get a very good idea of how big the tench in a given water grow, you are unlikely to be able to get a clear impression of how many there are. I would not, therefore, be disheartened if I only saw, say, a dozen fish. In fact I would be quite surprised if I saw many more; I would, however, be a bit concerned if I only saw 2 or 3, especially if weather conditions were good.

I mentioned that it should be possible to gauge their size, but be careful not to underestimate them because even really big fish do not look particularly impressive when seen from above. I have caught very many big tench so obviously I know what a big tench looks like, but I am constantly surprised at how unimpressive 6, 7 and even 8-pounders look when they are returned to the water. On the bank they look enormous, but viewed from above they look quite modest. Which makes me wonder just how big are those few fish that have made me gasp when I have seen them! Last August I saw the biggest tench I have ever seen—it was patrolling a stretch of bank between two fallen willows and despite watching it swimming to-and-fro in the crystal clear water for upwards of 20 minutes I found it impossible to gauge its size. It was an empty, post-spawned fish but could not, I am certain, have weighed less than 11 or 12 lb. I have, in the past, seen two other tench that might just possibly have topped double figures, but both of those were carrying

I return a seven-plus. I wonder why my sevens look so much bigger than a lot
of those we see in the weeklies . . .?

some spawn. That August specimen would, I believe, have comfortably exceeded double figures without the aid of spawn.

I often think about that fish and sometimes I doubt my judgement and wonder if I really saw what I think I saw. Even as I write these words I am wondering if the script has taken on a life of its own and if the fish was really as big as memory suggests—in a way, you see, I cannot recall the fish's dimensions, only the anecdote. But the anecdote is true—and I recall that when I saw the fish, it made me gasp in disbelief. I recall too that I watched it for a long while, and its size did not diminish under my scrutiny.

So, yes, I genuinely believe that it was every bit as large as I remember. But here is a paradox; I am not sure that I want to catch it. Well, part of me does, part of me would give just about anything to see that tench safely enfolded in the meshes of my landing net—and yet, where could my tench fishing go after the capture of such a fish? My perspectives would inevitably be changed—and my future tench trips would be devoid of a dream. If my dream became reality—what would replace it? And without a dream, where is the magic of it all?

But the specimen-hunter in me wants that fish, and wants it badly—so I shall fish for it.

If I succeed, I lose.

If I fail, I win.

But I have got to try.

Update

On arriving home from work today I learned that Kevin Maddocks of Beekay Publishers had telephoned to ask if I had a few more photographs because when the book was compiled it transpired that there were a few spare pages.

I rang him back and suggested that I do what I did with *Big Water Carp* and produce an 'Update' chapter. Kevin agreed that it would be a useful addition to the book ... mind you, his timing could have been better—I am boarding the ferry in less than 48 hour's time for a week's fishing in France, so the writing of this chapter is being sandwiched between bait-making, rig-tying, packing etc! So if my syntax is less scintillating than it might be, blame Kevin!

Winter Tench

Last winter (89/90) was exceptionally mild and water temperatures rarely fell below about 50°F (10°C). Predictably this led to some good tench fishing in some waters; but surprisingly the period after New Year was better than the period before. Normally I would expect November and December to be better than January and February—but last winter the reverse was the case. Why this should have been so, I have no idea. March was exceptional and, as regular readers of the angling Press will have noticed, a lot of big tench were taken from a wide variety of waters. Most of these, I suspect, were accidental captures by carp anglers—which leads me to wonder what would have been caught had tench received as much attention last March as they traditionally do in June. It is food for thought is it not?

Whether or not we will get another winter as mild as the last one is anyone's guess, although a lot of the weather-pundits are predicting that such will be the case, but if we do I for one will revise my opinion on the worth of winter tench fishing and will give them some serious attention. The experience of a couple of friends last winter suggests that midday to midnight is the best time—the second half of which can be adequately covered by after-work sessions. Think about it—no need for

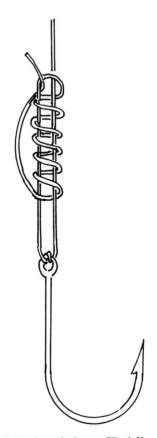

Twice-through-the-eye Clinch Knot.

pre-dawn starts, no competition for swims ... it has a lot to commend
it.

HPPE Hook-links

Kryston, the hook-link people, have put several new braids on the market
but to date I have not had the opportunity to test them. I used 'Silkworm'
virtually all last season though, and I am completely sold on it. It is,
without doubt, the best hook-link material I have ever used. When I
first started using it I experimented with knots tied with double-back
lengths of braid, but this resulted in rather bulky knots so I reverted
to my usual twice-through-the-eye Clinch Knot. I found that if I touched
the knot with a tiny drop of Superglue I got *at least* the breaking strain

claimed by Kryston for their product—and this with the knot tied in single, not double strand. I use a cocktail-stick to apply the glue incidentally, and I apply only the tiniest of tiny drops. If too much glue is used it runs along the braid by capillary action and makes it go stiff for a centimetre or two which, of course, defeats the object of using an ultra-soft link!

Initially I was a little worried that tangles might be a problem, but the use of up-line anti-tangle tube and a stringer makes tangles a rarity. The use of in-line leads (Zipp, Cruise etc) and anti-tangle tube eliminates them entirely, with or without stringers. I therefore use in-line leads most of the time and cannot honestly remember when I last had a tangled hook-link. Come to think of it—I doubt that I have had any tangles at all with this system.

A recent development may just possibly make the use of anti-tangle tube redundant. Dave Chilton of Kryston recently arranged for a sample of a liquid to be sent to me for testing. Dave describes it as an anti-tangle compound and when applied to Multi-strand or other loose-weave hook-link materials it slightly stiffens the material making it easier to handle and unlikely to tangle. The compound is best applied with finger and thumb and dries in approximately 60 seconds but, and here is the clever bit, within 60 seconds of immersion in water it completely dissolves allowing the Multi-strand (or other) link to revert to its original state. The compound is inert, odourless, non-toxic and non-volatile—and leaves no residues on a treated link. My tests with the material are as yet in their early stages and have been 'bench-tests' rather than practical fishing tests—but I will put the product through some extensive testing next week in France.

I suspect that its main use will be in 'taming' Multi-strand material. I do not think it is strictly necessary for braids because, frankly, with the terminal tackle I have described there are no problems associated with braids anyway—although it may interest those who use braids and believe that fish in really pressured waters are 'spooking' at the sight of anti-tangle tube.

Certainly it is an interesting product, but I shall reserve further comment until I have tested it properly—which unfortunately will be after this chapter has been sent off to the printer!

Reels

In Chapter Three (Tackle) when discussing reels I said that many of the current crop of new reels were somewhat out of proportion and were too big and heavy for my taste. They are ungainly too. But my objections were not solely aesthetic in that I am a confirmed back-winder and like to apply pressure to a running fish by finger pressure on the rear of the flier. This is no problem with reels of the Mitchell 410 type because the rear of the flier is smooth and free of obstructions; but few skirted-spool reels can be used in this way because their fliers either have finger-whacking protrusions, or their shape makes controlled finger pressure impossible. Since then, however, I have acquired some reels that have a nicely rounded back-edge to the flier that makes it perfect for the application of finger pressure. They are nicely proportioned reels too—and in their use to date show every indication of being extremely well engineered. They are from the DAM range and are long-spool, rear-drag models (the drag, incidentally, is excellent). I am currently using the CDi 240 for tench and the larger CD 150 for carp. I really cannot fault them—they are just about the most vice-less reels I have ever used. I am impressed.

Indicators

You will like this—I promise. Those of you who use monkey-climber indicators that have a wire loop at the top (as per Mickey Sly indicators) can increase the loading of the indicators by the simple expedient of pulling the loop from the indicator body (in the Sly model the loop is not glued in so it can be removed with a steady pull) and slipping a half-inch barrel-lead over one of the wire legs, then replacing the loop. If you want it heavier still, you slip another half-inch barrel-lead over the other leg. This gives you the advantage of a range of body-weights without it being necessary to carry (or buy!) a selection of same.

Be honest—it is a clever idea ... as befits the brother of the man who invented monkey-climbers in the first place!

Line-Aligner

Modesty inhibits me from claiming that this is the most efficient hooking arrangement yet devised ... no it doesn't, so I will! When I described it in the relevant section of the book it was still relatively new and although it had amply demonstrated its effectiveness I had yet to realise just *how* effective it could be. Brother Rick used it on one rod throughout the winter and matched it against his standard arrangement and at the last count the line-aligner was running at 100% as against about 65% for his standard rig (the percentages representing indicator movement converted to fish on the bank). This was with carp, but the principle holds good with tench too. In Rick's own words, or as near as I can recall without his letter to hand, 'It doesn't lead to more takes but it is certainly effective at converting takes to fish. Put simply—when the indicator moves, it's too late.'

The line-aligner is so effective that Rick did not want me to write

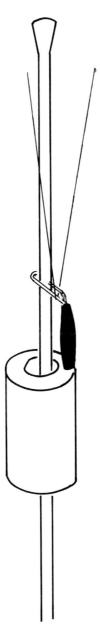

Mickey Sly indicator-body weighted with half-inch barrel-lead over one leg of wire loop.

about it—but as I explained to him, I get a bit tired of precocious 'wunder-kind' claiming other people's ideas as their own—or to be more precise, claiming *my* ideas as their own! To make matters worse, they usually do it in a blaze of tasteless, self-publicising 'hype'. Well, this is one idea they will *not* be able to claim ... my pathetic bid for immortality having now been recorded for posterity!

Frankly I doubt that the line-aligner will become used by very many people because it is a bit fiddly to tie—although there is always the possibility that Nashy will produce a ready-tied version in a bubble-pack!

Big Tench

If you read the 'comics' you will have doubtless seen that 'Fox Pool' (née Longfield) was recently netted by Leisure Sport, and living with the big carp was an 11-lb-plus tench! Being an April fish it was virtually devoid of spawn so its weight was not unnaturally enhanced in any way. I spoke to someone who held the fish in his arms and he said, 'I'm no tench angler so at first I did not fully appreciate what I was holding—then I took a good look at it and thought, Jesus H. Christ, this thing is incredibly enormous". Actually, he didn't say 'incredibly enormous', but in the interests of good taste, and having no wish to make reference to procreative activities in the after-life, I have paraphrased his comment!

And no—it did not get that big by eating carp anglers' boilies—if it had, it would have been caught repeatedly. But it wasn't. Even the regulars on the water were surprised when it appeared in the net.

Besides, if boilies make tench grow large, how come they have not had that effect on the Continent? Plenty of boilies go in some European waters, and have done so for a good many years, but the tench in those waters are like our's used to be. And there are plenty of waters in the UK that get an awful lot of boilies thrown in, but the tench remain relatively small.

I am in absolutely no doubt that the factors outlined in the 'Big Tench' chapter are the reason our tench grow so large. Something I did not mention but is doubtless relevant is that most of our gravel pits are in river valleys—and most of those rivers contain sewage—which in turn leads to phosphate contamination of the ground-water. The combination of nitrates and phosphates makes for a 'brew' that in moderation leads to greatly increased fertility, but when it occurs to excess it can lead to the proliferation of algae—and the presence of algae causes all sorts of problems associated with turbidity, oxygen levels and toxins.

The effects of enriching agents on our gravel-pits are currently working to our advantage—tench enthusiasts are currently enjoying a bit of a 'honeymoon' period ... but I am more than a little concerned about the future of the 'marriage'.

Post-script

In this section, as elsewhere in this book, I have mentioned certain products by name. Understandably some readers may suspect my motives and assume that I have some sort of financial interest in the sales of those products. This is not the case. I have no financial interest in any of the products nor any of the companies mentioned. I have, in fact, no tie-up or commercial connection with any manufacturer, distributor or retailer in the fishing tackle trade. My recommendations are therefore based on genuine enthusiasm and are not motivated by the prospect of any financial reward.

Index